The Magic
Of The Mind

How To Do What You
Want With Your Life

Louise Berlay

Published by Audio Enlightenment

Giving Voice to the Wisdom of the Ages

Printed in the United States of America

0 1 2 3 4 5 6 7 8 9

First Printing, 2017

ISBN 978-1-941489-32-1

www.MetaphysicalPocketBooks.Com

The Magic of the Mind

Is now available on iTunes in the spoken word

First "AudioEnlightenmentPress.Com" Printing
August, 2017

I dedicate this work
to my beloved son
Neville

Introduction

Introduction by the Author's Son

As my mother liked to say, it's hard being a prophet in your own land. I'd have to agree, based on feelings I had about her during my teens and young adulthood. Today, at sixty-five, I see her not as a prophet, but as a fully human, courageous, and resourceful woman balancing demands of family, household, and a deep, spiritual calling.

Stories my mother told of her early life suggest that calling was present long before she could name it. Later, it found expression in close friendship and study with a first, spiritual teacher, Neville Goddard. His lectures and books helped inspire what she called her homework - the regular practice of focused, joyful reverie described in these pages. As you'll read, such reverie led to the fulfillment of a long succession of life goals.

My mother's beginnings were quite humble. Born during the depression on a farm in rural Oklahoma, she left home early, and with her younger sister, Gerry, moved to Tucson, Arizona; in her twenties, she met and married a building-contractor, worked at his side, and learned to operate heavy, earth-moving machinery; during leisure hours, she and her husband set up a trapeze-bar in a large warehouse, practiced flying and catching maneuvers; later, my mother learned to fly a plane, and with the advent of war, became the first woman in Arizona welding parts for fighter-planes.

I learned of my mother's time as a welder a few months after her death, when my Aunt Gerry sent me a few, brittle pages from a 1942 issue of Look magazine. The feature they contained, part human-interest story, part war-propaganda, showed my mother on the job in a welder's helmet, lit blow-torch in hand. Other shots had her in a swim-suit, frolicking with a puppy, or playing the accordion, or in the tub, under billowing soap bubbles... Why had she never mentioned the feature? Possibly, because it portrayed a time in her life, a version of herself with which she no longer identified.

Once or twice, she spoke to me of restlessness in her first marriage, and at work; of how she longed for a life of greater depth and meaning. She spoke with sadness of asking her husband for a divorce; described his hurt, and eventual agreement.

With Gerry, she moved to Los Angeles, took a job as a bank-teller, began studying with Neville, and soon after, met a fine-art dealer who hired her as an assistant. Through these transitions, I suspect her beauty was an asset, and may have opened many doors.

In the early 1960's, when my brother and I were young teenagers, she was given a book on Buddhist thought; soon, she began formal sitting practice at a Zen Buddhist center near our home in Manhattan. That discipline led to extended meditation retreats, then to mystical experience described in this book. Combining new insight with the practice of directed imagination, she began teaching a weekly class, and eventually wrote The Magic of the Mind.

May her book serve you well. May it be a doorway to realms of joyful imagination, and an ally in uncovering the mind and heart of love.

- Neville Berle

August, 2017

Contents

Acknowledgments

The merit in this book is due to those whom I have long studied and to the many noble hearts who have lovingly enhanced my life.

I am ever grateful to my late and beloved husband who was my idol and inspiration... To our fine son Neville whom I love and admire and who enriches my life... And to my extended family each of whom is deeply imprinted in my heart.

Our closest friends "Neville," (mystical philosopher- teacher-author) and his family who were treasures beyond price and sorely missed.

Dorothy Gilbert was priceless in assisting my New York lectures on this subject and will always have her own special place in my heart.

Cavett Robert, well-loved modern sage of Phoenix, Arizona, and founder of the National Speakers Association has been a great source of guidance and inspiration.

In this second edition, I thank my dear friend Don Ginn of La Jolla, California for his great kindness to me, and whom I hear from his followers is a masterful teacher in his seminars for fulfilling the dreams of our heart and determining our chosen destiny.

I am ever grateful to Glenn Roberts for his special kindness, his generous and best of all gifts: his time and personal efforts on my behalf and for his unsurpassed nobility of the heart.

Lesley Davison, glorious spirit of light and love, in addition to her own busy schedule has lovingly taken on the multiple efforts of republishing this new edition of my work.

To these and others who believe in me, my loving thanks.

Preface

Greetings dear reader . . .

Ralph Waldo Emerson author, lecturer, poet and transcendentalist was one of the greatest influences on American thought. Among his idealistic words of wisdom was this concept: "The only gift is a portion of thyself."

In this light, I offer you the best and kindest of my thoughts and hope to be admitted into the inner sanctuary of your own.

I studied the Creative Process from among the wisest minds of whom there is any record. This enabled me to fulfill all my goals. Now, I am committed to sharing this knowledge in order that you too, may benefit from their wisdom.

What more could we ask, dear fellow wayfarer than to open our mind to one another, unless, perhaps, wonder should smile upon my effort and you should also accept my love.

Louise Berlay

Important

To be successful Review this Page Daily

Is Your Desire Morally Justified?

Set aside a minimum of 15 to 30 minutes the first thing after waking and the last thing at night to create and fulfill your desires.

Don't Try and Make it Happen

Your desires will materialize as soon as you have embodied and rehearsed it until it has sufficient energy to move from imagination to the outer world of your experience.

1. Happily Assume that Fulfillment is present.

2. Silently rehearse in happy Imagination that which would naturally "Follow" its presence; Daily, do in your mind that which you would be doing had it already occurred.

3. Silently tell everyone close to you about its ideal conditions

4. During every free moment, silently and joyfully act out in your mind, its natural consequences, feel and wear your new self image.

The Creative Process

Today's dream is tomorrow's reality.

William Shakespeare

I invite you to come with me if you will, and let us explore together the creative nature of our mind.

In the subtleties of universal law lie the principles and processes of creation. And we, multiple expressions of a single reality, are immersed in an infinite ocean of dynamic energy that awaits our command. Does it not follow that after survival, our first priority should be to learn the nature of the laws that govern our lives? And where better to begin than in our mind?

Actually, these laws and processes have been known since ancient times, but only to the few. For thousands of years, long preceding recorded history, the wisest men of the world taught their small groups of followers that which our modern science has learned only in recent times: that the creative process is activated by our beliefs, assumptions, and self-identification, as well as imagination in its various aspects such as fantasy and daydreams.

Shakespeare revealed this insight in his observation, "Imagination bodies-forth the forms of things." He knew that all forms and all things are brought into being through this natural and magical process he utilized so extensively, imagination.

"Whatsoever things you desire, 'believe' you have received them, and they shall be yours," instructs a biblical passage.

An ancient Chinese sage whose name is lost in antiquity taught: "Daydream in the ultimate you desire to obtain." And his revered countryman, the humble Lao-Tzu, distilled this thought even further in his

1

succinct advice: "The best way to do is 'to be.'" Centuries later and across the world, Meister Eckart, the German mystical theologian, expressed the same insight: "Leave off doing that you may 'be.'"

In other words, we should choose our role in life and act it out in our mind until it becomes established in the outer world. Whether it is a single desire or a destiny, we are advised to accept it as present in the here and now. This was well stated by the watchword of the late 1960s, "Be there."

The late Dr. Carl Jung, world famous Swiss psychologist, explained: "Without the play of 'fantasy,' no creation has ever come into being."

The Creative Process has been long and well understood, but only by a few. Some five hundred years B.C. the great East Indian Buddha taught: 'What we are is the result of all that we have thought." Across the world the 19th-century English literary figure William Henley stated a similar human potential: "I am the master of my fate, I am the captain of my soul."

But, dear reader, this mastery cannot occur without our knowledge of its processes. Though it is seldom realized, we are innately endowed with all the necessary faculties for becoming true masters of our life and destiny.

So please think of it, dear friend—what would most enrich your life? What would make you the happiest and benefit all whom it would affect? If it is in harmony with the natural order of life, and if you wish it, I would be honored to help you to attain it, and stay by your side, if you like, every step of the way.

Let us observe together this magical process with which we are richly empowered. It is composed of three simple elements:

1. Idea (or definition)

2. Assumption, and

3. Imaginal experience

The laws of the mind are as precise and dependable as those of mathematics or gravity. So until each aspect of this governing law is met, there can be no fulfillment of our desire.

As taught by the wisest of men, "belief" is surely the greatest activator of the creative process. But in the matter of an unrealized desire, belief does not merely happen, it does not initiate itself; it must grow and develop from "the roots of assumption." So how, dear friend, do we invoke belief? By a discipline of repeated practice—rehearsing the happy results and consequences of our desire as though it were already fulfilled.

Do in your imagination that which you would be doing were it already realized. Embody the joy which would naturally accompany its presence. By sustaining this daily practice, its energy-pattern, its mental blueprint, if you will, becomes increasingly energized until it is well established, until it becomes a strongly imprinted subconscious habit. At this point it is the nature of the process to reflect or project our blueprint from its subjective, inner domain to the objective outer world of our experience. In this daily repetition we become so familiar with the results that we are enabled to "believe."

The biblical teaching of "whatsoever you desire, believe that you *have received"* also implies that if we believe in something as having already occurred, we would naturally think and act accordingly, that we would be faithful to our belief.

Is it not clear that if we are following the instruction as given, we cannot continue to pray and ask for it, but rather follow through in the silence of our mind with that which would be its natural consequence?

Unlike the delusion of our senses, creation does not and cannot possibly occur in the outside world. Creation is always from the subjective to the objective. Our sight misleads us into believing that some great structure is being created in the outer world of our perception, yet we know that it was first built in the mind. That which we observe is the follow-through. There is no other way: creation is subjective cause. The finished product is objective effect.

Someone noted amusingly that there are three kinds of people: those who make things happen, those who watch things happen, and those who have no idea what happened. Actually, we all belong to the first group, "those who make things happen," but with an important difference: we have made our present conditions happen, some of which we may have preferred not to occur. Life does not fulfill our wishes, it fulfills our dominant thought patterns.

So think of it, dear friend; is there something important missing in your life? Is there something which needs to be resolved? Is it a matter of relationships? The right job or career? Even if you do not know what you want, in the practice of "disciplined silence" you can find the ideal vocation or path for which you are best suited and in which you can make a meaningful contribution to life. By rehearsing a scene in which you silently celebrate your ideal occupation and engage in imaginary conversations to this effect, your subconscious will not only find and reflect it in your conscious mind, but it will be perfect for you in every way. Be sure to refer to it always as "ultimately perfect and ideal."

Please think of your own desire and come with me, if you will, into my secret dreams and observe the creative process in action.

I was in love with the world of fine art and desired to work effectively in this field. I wanted to travel broadly on the largest ships and planes, visit the greatest cities and wonders of the world. I was eager to see the many famous museums and to enjoy in the original the great masterpieces that I had studied. Yet, among all these pleasures something seemed to be missing; not knowing exactly what, I called it my

4

"Undefined Wonder." Totally ignorant of the laws of the mind, I merely wished and hoped, and my desires remained unfulfilled.

Finally, I began to look for the reasons and learned that wishing and hoping have no power of fulfillment. At last I learned of the creative process of the mind, and committed myself to a nightly practice of constructive new mental habits. In imagination, I worked joyfully and effectively in the field of fine art. In my mind I did all that I assumed I would be doing were it already realized. I fantasized that my room was a lovely, private stateroom aboard ship where I traveled far and wide. In imagination, I smelled the salt air over the ocean, saw and heard the white seagulls flying overhead. In my mind, I met lovely people, dined with several charming men, promenaded on deck with the ship's officers and danced the nights away all across the Atlantic. In Europe, I thrilled at the famous museums and enjoyed a variety of social activities. And I finished each dream rehearsal silently celebrating my undefined wonder. And so vividly and happily did I embody all the sensations and tones of reality that after only three weeks of faithful nightly practice and without a word to anyone or any outward effort whatever, suddenly I was offered an elegant position in the field of fine art. And I worked with a collection of Renaissance masters, including Rembrandt and Leonardo da Vinci.

Then one day my employer came to me and announced that something very important was about to occur in the field of great paintings and he needed to send me to Europe for five weeks, all expenses paid. Imagine my joy. Soon I was actually in my lovely private stateroom, traveling first class and round trip on the two largest ships afloat. Everything was a delight.

The dining room steward, with no knowledge of my creative dream rehearsals, actually seated me with three charming gentlemen, two of whom owned important New York art galleries and the third of whom was an Italian movie producer returning home from Hollywood. Two of the ship's officers in their impeccable white uniforms, unaware that I had been walking with them in my dreams, invited me for a daily promenade on deck. One of them invited me on a tour of the ship, which included descending into the hold on narrow vertical ladders to see the mysterious engine room with its enormous motors that empowered this majestic, floating city. It was mind-expanding and fascinating to see, especially with such a handsome and attentive officer as my guide. They taught me to say ship, not boat, and to make U-turns navy-style. The evenings were great fun and with several gallant partners I danced all across the Atlantic.

Arriving in Paris in the evening, I was lavishly wined and dined in one of the city's most famous restaurants, where course after course of gourmet masterpieces seemed never ending. The following day I was invited to a private sit-down luncheon for fourteen. Knowing that it was to be another sumptuous affair of the table, my stomach protested two such extravaganzas in succession. So I tried to decline, but my gracious hosts refused to accept my regrets and I attended unwillingly.

It is important to note that after we have rehearsed a mental pattern until it is well established and highly energized, it will objectify in our experience unless we choose to revise it.

In imaginal experience, I had firmly recorded in my subconscious some "Undefined Wonder" that I assumed had already occurred during my five-week trip. In keeping with the dependable laws and powers of cause and effect, my subconscious mind found the means to manifest this wonder. So even against my wishes, I was caused to attend the luncheon where the wonder did, in fact, occur. But more of this later.

Among the many pleasures of my trip was seeing the highlights of Paris, London and Rome, as well as the storybook city of Venice, Marseilles and the Isle of Capri. Fulfilling the main purpose of my trip, I strolled leisurely through the famous museums, savoring many of my favorite works of art.

I assure you that every detail I rehearsed in "the inner domain of causes" was experienced in "the outer world of effects." And the continued practice of my waking dreams resulted in some fifty deluxe trips from the Far East to the Far West, as well as much more important things: an ideal marriage, our fine son Neville, and a beautiful and enriching life together.

Yes, experience is the mirror of our mind, and our dominant thought patterns are the blueprints of tomorrow.

We live as we dream.

—Joseph Conrad

The Subconscious Mind

Our life is what our thoughts have made it.

— Marcus Aurelius

One of the greatest mysteries of our mental faculties is that of our subconscious mind. As our awareness is outwardly focused, it has no perception of its interacting counterpart functioning below the threshold of its horizon. Conjointly, conscious and subconscious form a single, unified faculty: our mind.

Modern science is now discovering these secrets that have been hidden to all but the greatest contemplative sages of the world who observed their function in the deepest silence of "direct knowing."

It is awesome that this elusive faculty spontaneously records the total experience of our lives. There are numerous documented accounts of those confronting their final exits—from accidents, near drowning, surgery and the like—who unexpectedly recovered and told of having either reviewed or re-experienced all aspects of their entire lives complete with the emotion. The traumatic survival alert causes powerful stimulants to be released into the organism that unite the subconscious with the conscious.

The myriad encoded "imprints" from our past, from benign to alarming, interacting in this mysterious repository are the source of our character, moods, personality, and the ongoing quality of our experience. Those prone to sickness, accident, and failure continue to act out their unconscious and unhealthy self-programming.

Sri Yukteswar, the East Indian enlightened spiritual teacher, wrote, "You have made yourself unwell. You indispose yourself. It is your thoughts that have made you feel alternately weak and strong."

Yes, my dear, to the degree that our thoughts are in harmony with the natural ebb and flow of life, we are healthy, well balanced and peaceful. Conversely, our suffering is the result of thoughts in discord.

Such basic and essential knowledge will one day be taught in the early years of school.

It could be rightly said that the quality of our unconscious programming stored away in the vast archives of our subconscious mind is the quality of our person, our present and our future.

Happily, the opportunity is always present for us to become masters of our fate by a discipline of regrooming our thought patterns. It is a simple process and can be accomplished within a few weeks without assistance. No one need know of your practice. All that it requires is from fifteen-to-thirty minutes a day of constructive and pleasant imaginal experience until all your thoughts are of a positive and enhancing nature.

We should not try to stop doing something undesirable, for our attention will further energize and sustain it. We should replace it with a healthy and desirable thought pattern.

Generally, we associate the conscious level of our mind, together with our body, as being our whole person. We have notions about a subconscious, but for the most part we are unaware that our perception, and the knowledge we have acquired are but the smallest part of our mind. As with all other aspects of our being, our mind is multi-tiered: the conscious aspect is similar to the visible surface of the iceberg, while the main body is below the level of our perception.

Just as it is not necessary to be a mechanic to drive a car, neither is it required to know more about our subconscious mind than is useful to succeed with our purpose. We do not usually consider its function in connection with our desires, but it would be wise to keep in mind that it records all our mental and emotional experience just as impersonally as a camera and recorder; that it has an automatic replay that works independently of our perception, and that our present experience or its equivalent was "recorded earlier."

Reprogramming our subconscious is a great way to free ourselves from an undesirable habit or to establish a new one. If it is your desire to stop smoking, overdrinking, overspending, or gambling for example, it is unwise to try to succeed by will power, which causes stress and discomfort and is less likely to be effective. The same is true for over or undereating, over or underreacting, or any other undesirable habit-will power is not the best way.

As stated elsewhere, everything has its price, and in this regard it is very small indeed to spend as little as a few minutes a day to program your subconscious with that which is desirable, but the exercise should be regular and at the same time if possible.

It is helpful to note on a calendar or write in a book each time you complete your mental exercise, as the visible record of your investment in time builds confidence in your discipline and adds energy to your project.

In all your practice be sure to check and recheck your attitude and be certain that you are viewing your accomplishment as already present, and that your imaginal experience is of that which would naturally follow. Your programming must begin at the end result; you must stand on the foundation of its having already occurred, then embody the great feeling this would invoke and sustain it throughout your silent practice time.

You will amaze yourself with one achievement after another, all rooted in integrity, and all enriching your life.

> Whatever is true, whatever is honorable,
> whatever is just, whatever is pure,
> whatever is lovely, whatever is gracious,
> if there is any excellence,

if there is anything worthy of praise,
think about these things.

—Philippians 4:8

Sports

You cannot fail if you see yourself as successful.

John Scott

Are you a golfer, bowler or tennis buff? Are you involved in any active sport? If so, and if you are not already using the creative process in your game, somebody else will be and this will give them an enormous advantage. So come closer and listen carefully to that which the wisest of men have said about the laws of our mind.

All fulfillment of our desires must pass through the gates of imagination, there is no other entrance. If we would improve our game it is essential that we open our mind to the creative powers at our disposal.

We can never achieve our highest potential if we depend only upon our intellect and its limited knowledge. It is not unlike a great airport with its thoughts arriving and taking off in all directions. Even at best, it is sensitive to myriad distractions, and is unable to access perfectly every changing situation and follow through with reliable accuracy.

Miraculously, we have powers that can do precisely that. Sportsmen of the Far East, certainly the winners, have known and practiced for many centuries some form of "silent time" in which they rehearsed in the creative powers of imagination not how to improve their skill, but "winning the game."

The great sages became great not through intellectual brilliance, but by disciplined silence, which has access to all knowledge. As the result of their profound insight into the causes of things, they taught their followers the mental discipline of fixing their attention upon the ultimate fulfillment of their desire, experiencing it over and over again in their imagination until it became strongly imprinted in their subconscious mind.

The greatest motivating force is desire and the greatest implementing force is imagination. This activates the creative forces in its own likeness.

So what is the ultimate of your desire? It is not the way you hit the ball or any other single aspect of your game. It is "winning" the game. This is the ultimate goal and this should be the single, one-pointed focus of your attention.

By rehearsing the ultimate, you are self-programming your subconscious mind to perform in consistent perfection, whatever the circumstances. The conscious mind is not capable of all that is encompassed in such accuracy. But the subconscious, which has no faculty of reason or logic, performs its natural function of recording our imaginal experience in the degree of energy and emotion with which we have endowed it. When, by repetition of our practice this subliminal experience is sufficiently charged and energized, when it has become a strongly imprinted habit pattern, it is the nature of the subconscious to project this mental blueprint into the outer world of our experience.

This is the process and source of all our experience, though most of it is initiated unconsciously. Here, it is shown how to set in motion those causes which will result in our desired effect.

Your silent practice should consist of happy variations on the single theme of "winning" the game. And you will achieve your purpose sooner if you observe two vitally important ingredients in the formula for success.

1. Rehearse all silent practice in the highest joy of which you are capable.

2. Begin at the ultimate by assuming that your desire is already realized. You have already won the game or tournament and are now joyfully celebrating your victory.

If there is a trophy, touch it in your mind, feel its substance, its weight, its reality. If it is a check, visualize in your mind's eye the clear figures beside the dollar sign. Feel its texture; sense the explosion of excitement. Shake the hand from which it was offered. Hear the applause and the raves. See it on the printed page. Hear the voices of your friends confirming your victory and watch it on T.V.

In this subjective practice of "winning" you will activate higher laws beyond the reach of knowledge and reason. You will transcend the "hit-and-miss" of conscious effort and vibrate on the planes of victory.

One of the few greatest chess players of the world, Alexander Alekheine, vanquished his opponents with unequaled diversity and manipulation and was able to play a couple of dozen adversaries simultaneously and win. This was due not only to playing the game in his mind, which is common practice, but the fact that he regularly rehearsed winning in his mind.

Alex Morrison, renowned golf pro, taught his pupils to golf mentally in their easy chairs. Doing so, Lew Lehr broke ninety for the first time with no outside practice at all.

Science does not know its debt to imagination.

— Ralph Waldo Emerson

The Magic of the Mind

Cause and Effect

Our Attitudes determine our altitudes

— A.P. Gouthey

Dear friend, it is not enough merely to write; my purpose is to help you harmonize and enhance your life. That is, if you wish it. And if so, please allow me to come into your thoughts daily by turning to these pages, even for a single idea, before beginning "your silent time." For it is very much more effective if we can find a note of inspiration to lift our spirits as we fly away with that elusive bird called "imagination."

Look for sources of inspiration on every side, a book, a poem, a lovely piece of music, flowers, a glorious sunrise or sunset, an entrancing sky, or anything that lifts your spirits. This sets the tone of your enriching adventure in the inner domain of "imaginal experience."

Let us look at some fascinating facts.

• Cause must precede effect. Effect is the mirror of cause.

• It is against all the laws of the universe that something should occur without a cause. Things and conditions cannot initiate themselves.

• All experiences and circumstances are objective effects of subjective causes.

• In our human condition, either knowingly or unknowingly, by commission or omission, we initiate the causes of our experience by our dominant thought patterns, beliefs, and attitudes.

After becoming aware of the creative nature of our thoughts, I set about regrooming my own mental habits. I became more and more alert to the quality of my expressions and recognized them as *the subjective causes of my conditions and circumstances.* I saw that many of them reflected unconscious negative attitudes that I had absorbed since childhood. Expressions such as "that's just my luck," "wouldn't you know that would happen," "I knew it wouldn't work,"—these and others like them are powerfully destructive, *for our thought patterns are the blueprints of our experience.*

Begin to survey your attitudes as they are reflected in your speech and you will see the causes of the conditions of your life. Many times I found myself half way through a negative statement when I recognized it and stopped, finishing with no, I don't want to say that. One lady said that when replacing her negatives with positives, as soon as she recognized the destructive element of her words she quickly added, "cancel," and reversed her remark.

We must become conscious of our thoughts, attitudes and speech habits before we can begin to replace them with those which will produce the desired effect. Even thought patterns to which we have been long-conditioned can be revised within only a few weeks by becoming aware and alert to their quality.

Any undesirable condition is a signal that we are sustaining it by the mental habits from which it derives its energy. Unless we change the cause, the effect will continue.

Please do not try forcefully to stop a habit, for attention energizes its object. This creates a stressful conflict as force is met with resistance. We should neither resist nor pursue; rather, quietly and happily accept the ideal condition and proceed normally from there.

If you are not already doing so, you will find it growth-promoting to observe others, their positions, conditions and speech habits. You will come to recognize the cause in the effect. You will see people as self-programmed states of "consciousness in action." This is not judgmental, but discerning. Discernment makes no judgment of the person, but perceives the circumstances as that of subjective conditioning.

To one who has developed this insight, everything about ourselves shouts who and what we are, how we feel about ourselves and our degree of self-worth. Our eyes and glances, our changing facial expressions and responses, our posture, hands, gestures, our tones and manner of speech; all these plus the subtleties of all that we radiate, comprise the quality and caliber of our presence. Emerson said it marvelously, "What you are thunders so that I cannot hear what you say..." Knowing this, what should be the nature of our response? We should identify with, "embody" as in the present, all that we admire and aspire to be. As quoted elsewhere, William James noted, "Act the part and you will become the part."

So, if we would be healthy, happy and fulfilled, it is essential that we learn the principles, laws and processes of that all-important and magical pair, "cause and effect."

If you will create the cause, the effect will take care of itself. In the Far East this might be equated with the oxcart: the ox being the cause, and the wheel tracks being the effect.

So, do not concern yourself with the effect of your desire. Rather, be faithful to your daily practice and try to extend your self-identification and sense of fulfillment (with all its joy) to longer and longer periods throughout the day until your new role in life becomes permanently established.

Are you ready, my friend, to take responsibility for the events and circumstances of your life? If not yet, you will come to see that we are self-made—products of our own thoughts.

And if there is anything we would change, it must begin with a change in our thoughts.

Cause and effect equals reward and punishment. If our thoughts and actions promote life, harmony, greater knowledge, healthy progress and prosperity, we are self-rewarded. If we violate the natural order of life and the inherent rights of others, we are self-punished.

There is no more worthy endeavor than to learn the natural laws of our mind which are impersonal and self-initiated. There is no one rewarding or punishing us for our actions. We invoke the quality of the result by the quality of the cause we set in motion. It is all a matter of activating, by our thoughts and actions, natural laws which are in harmony with life and the well-being of all whom they affect. Knowingly or unknowingly, by commission or omission, we are self-rewarded and self-punished.

In regard to experience and circumstance being the mirror of our mind, it could be reasonably asked, how am I responsible for this or that accident, illness, misfortune? I did nothing to cause it. The question is simple but the answer, complex, in that the cause is likely to be lost in a chain of domino effects concerning the influences of our inherited genes, our early and unconscious conditioning and our own self-programming. Add to this our changing frequencies, wavelengths, polarity and other interacting forces. All these create a predisposition toward that which is in harmony or in conflict with the natural order of life.

This week a scientific statement was released to the effect that the buildings in Mexico City which were demolished in the recent earthquake were in the same frequency as that of the earthquake. The others were untouched.

Unless our lives are planned, organized and moving directly toward our goals, we are weaving back and forth across the speeding freeway of life.

We must have a purpose, a clearly defined project, and keep to our direction. If we don't know what we want or how to begin, we can still succeed very well with the following practice—it is simple, easy and powerfully creative. It takes very little time, but it must be done regularly, as in keeping the fire burning to keep the tea kettle boiling.

First, we "activate a desirable cause"; effect takes care of itself. Sit comfortably. Relax. Close your eyes.

1. Think of someone and visualize them in perfect harmony in every possible way. See them ultimately ideal, active, fulfilled and radiantly healthy and happy. Hold this vision about two minutes.

You have just made the highest possible gift, a portion of yourself. You have activated a beautiful and highly creative cause for another. You are of noble spirit for you are a divine being.

2. In the silence of your mind imagine that you are engaged in something undefined but useful and beneficial to all whom it concerns.

You are wonderfully enriched and fulfilled. Life is beautiful and you feel marvelous in its free-flowing harmony. Hold three to five minutes.

Practice night and morning the same two steps, and don't look for results. "Assume" they are present. Be happy, be light and be smiling and you will have much to smile about. I visualize you in the same ultimate ideal.

If you think you can, or you think you can't, you are right.

— **Henry Ford**

Out of the Blue

Enjoy to the fullest the resources that are within thy reach

— Pindar

For years I have talked with Gerry and Gary, my endearing sister and brother in law, about the creative process of our mind and how it reproduces our mental habits. We spoke about wishing for something, but holding the attitude of its absence and lack, thus giving crossed signals to the creative process in our subconscious mind. And how wishing is itself a negative, as "our habitual thoughts and attitudes are highly creative and PERPETUATE THEMSELVES in our experience"

We discussed the fact that whatever is predominate in our thoughts is the direction of our lives, and that wittingly or unwittingly we are each, thought by thought, shaping and molding the quality of our own destiny. We observed the lives of various people and saw their attitudes corresponded with their experience. Whether happy or disenchanted, well or ill, financially affluent or depressed, we noted the cause equals effect.

We remarked that young children should be taught in school the tremendous importance of the creative process of their minds and how to create sustain a healthy and productive mental attitude.

During one of these conversations in which we shared our most recent successes of the creative laws of our mind, Gary remarked that he had never engaged in a discipline of imaginal experience to demonstrate increased finances. He suggested to my sister Gerry that they choose a figure and invest some daily creative time toward this goal. She liked the idea and they settled on a figure of $150,000.

They had fulfilled other goals; why should the creative process not work for money as well? Knowing that this meant engaging in a

23

discipline of well stipulated creative time, in which they must rehearse the consequences of their desire as already realized and endow it with life by "feeling," they resolved to make it a very serious project. Carefully following all the rules, the most important of which was sustaining a sense of joy and celebration about the results of their fulfillment, they set out on their inward journey.

The story follows as the two related it to me in happy animation.

"We felt that our energies were highest in the morning, so we decided to do our creative rehearsals the first thing after waking, and sitting rather than lying, in order to remain awake and alert. So, we began and found it to be both easy and pleasant to imagine that we were experiencing really fun things and places that we both enjoy. We got off to a good start and agreed that we would give the project our very best and faithful attention.

"Assuming that this additional $150,000 was already added to our investments, we chose to increase our travels to new and exciting horizons. Having enjoyed several cruises, we selected another direction and imagined that we were on a long voyage. While sitting in the big lounge chairs at home in our den, we each surrounded ourselves with the impression of an imaginary ship. Entirely forgetting where we actually sat, we experienced in sensory detail a variety of pleasant activities. We felt ourselves in our attractive stateroom and engaged in conversations about the pleasures of the trip. When we went to bed at night in our own apartment, we imagined that we were aboard ship, that we felt the slight motion of the waves, and we thought of home as being in the opposite direction of our travel.

'We looked for inspiration from books, music and selected television programs wherever possible, as we found that our rehearsal of our 'dream come true' felt more real and was more pleasurable when we began on a happy note.

"Realizing the benefit of directing our highest energies of the day into our creative practice, we spoke to no one about our project. We find that all our plans work out best when we talk about them only after they happen.

"After one month of daily practice we felt that our goal had been fully conceived and that it was now forming and developing in our subconscious. We spoke very little about it to one another, just a few words to communicate our bright spirit and our teamwork. At the end of the second month we noticed a broader perspective in our attitude about our financial security. It seemed that we had grown and expanded mentally. But there were no signs of any change.

"We invested our time in a third month and at the end of this time there were signs, but not the ones we counted on. Both of us had begun to weary a bit, and doubts crept in as to whether or not our dream investment would ever pay any dividends. Yet, neither of us wanted to admit this to the other, nor even to ourselves. Feeling somewhat discouraged, we continued our daily practice and I found myself rehearsing new scenes to enliven the routine. Neither of us had made any decision as to how long we would continue our rehearsals, but we knew that we were not ready to give up. Now, we had reached the end of our fourth month of creative imagining with the only sign of change being that of our drooping spirits. Still we withheld discussing it, as each of us felt it would discourage the other one.

"We both wondered if the magnitude of one's desire might influence the time required for it to develop in the creative subconscious and move from the subjective to the objective domain. Did money not represent its equivalent in energy? Perhaps we had not fulfilled the requirement for the money we had accepted as being already ours. We wondered how a higher or lower figure might have affected our practice. Would one thousand dollars have been easier to demonstrate than one million, for example?

"As we each wrestled silently with such questions, we realized that we had made a four-month investment of daily practice time and were faced with the beginning of a fifth month. What should we do? Should we stop the rehearsals and assume that our subconscious was sufficiently imprinted and would objectify our plan in due time, or should we continue until either it appeared or it became clear that something was missing in our practice?

"At this point the phone rang and an unfamiliar voice asked to speak to Gary. From the tone it was clearly long distance. Watching Gary with curiosity about the identity of the caller, I noticed that suddenly his face became flushed and his eyes widened in surprise. From his answers it was evident that he was being asked to identify himself very thoroughly.

Was it possible? Could it be? Did I dare to hope that this was the great moment of truth? Gary hung up the phone and shouted excitedly, 'That's it! That's our $150,000, right out of the blue.'

"We both hugged, laughed and danced around the room exclaiming, 'It worked, it actually happened.' 'And we'll have the money within a few weeks,' said Gary.

"Well, it came, as you know, and the check was even more than we expected. After taxes, we received $167,000."

"But what was its source," I asked, "the lottery, a tax refund, the winning of a contest, or the horse races?"

"Nothing of the kind," they answered excitedly. "It was from the last source you could possibly imagine."

"Do you mean," I queried, "that it was something that you could never have expected?"

"Never in a million years," they assured me.

All this occurred only recently and you can well imagine that their $150,000 is now well invested and that they are reserved on another exciting cruise to exotic places.

Inspired by their successful efforts, they are now working on a new project and plan to continue one after another.

Man is truly in his element when he is in the process of creation. When he ceases to be creative, he declines. It could be said that life and living is a continual creative process.

Gary, speaking words of wisdom, announced, "If only people knew that they can fulfill their own dreams by living in them in the present."

The subconscious is the womb of creation.
Whatever the mind of man can conceive and feel as true;
the subconscious can and must objectify.

— Neville Goddard

The Magic of the Mind

Man: Natural Born Creator

Success or Failure is caused more by mental attitude
than by mental capacities

— Dr. Walter Scott
President, Northwestern University

As thought is creative and perpetuates its own likeness, we are natural and inherent creators throughout our lives. After survival, there is nothing as vitally important to our well-being as that of learning the effects of our thoughts. As this knowledge is still not widely known, most of us were taught in "negatives" instead of "positives." It was "don't forget," instead of "remember to"—thus programming two negatives and setting the stage for a poor memory. We were told, "you're going to catch your death of cold," instead of "wear your coat and stay warm." In this manner, our destructive thought patterns are passed down through the generations. This is reflected in alarming rates of illness and undesirable behavior.

We should become keenly alert to the quality of our thoughts and know that they are creating their very likeness in our experience.

As natural-born creators, we should groom our attitudes, which are thought patterns that have become habitual. Attitudes are emotionally charged, living, active forces that constantly reflect their qualities in our lives.

We do not normally think of ourselves as creators. We do not recognize that all our mental activity is perpetuating its quality and creating our destiny.

Though the true nature of life is mystical, for all practical purposes it could be rightly said that life is for growth and enrichment. And the more we can learn of our creative nature, the brighter and more fulfilled will be our lives.

29

The Magic of the Mind

In the creative state a man is taken out of himself.
He lets down, as it were, a bucket into his subconscious,
and draws up something which is normally beyond his reach.
He mixes this thing with his normal experiences,
and out of the mixture he makes a work of art.

— E.M. Forster

Cavett Robert's Human Engineering

The ability to deal with people is as purchasable a commodity as
sugar or coffee, and I pay more for that ability than for any
other under the sun.

— John D. Rockefeller

J.J. didn't like his job. Every morning he went to work down in spirit,
dragging his feet and dreading another boring day.

He thought about how easy and unencumbered his life had been
before he saddled himself with a family. If only he had waited until he
could afford its heavy responsibilities. Hindsight was so much clearer
than foresight.

More and more he hated to go to work. It was affecting all aspects of
his life. His energy was low, his digestion wasn't working and he slept
poorly. Its influence was also reflected in his wife and children. His wife
was becoming estranged and intimacy was no longer welcome in the
bedroom.

One day he was called to his boss's office to be told that his services
were not an asset to the company. He had lost his job.

The bottom had fallen out. How could he tell his wife? She wouldn't
understand. How he hated to go home.

Now followed months of job rejection—devastating to his confidence
and self-esteem. His life declined on all fronts and J.J. despaired of ever
resolving his problems.

Then one day there was a call from one of his friends at his former
job who knew of his plight and who announced that the company had
engaged some famous man named Cavett Robert to teach a seminar on

success with people through human engineering. He asked J.J. to sit-in on the lectures with him.

J.J. was not interested and found every excuse not to attend. His friend persisted and at last he agreed to go-

At the seminar, J.J. was stirred by the clarity, wisdom, spirit and dynamism of Mr. Robert. The man spoke so eloquently from his heart that everyone present felt that he was determined that each of them should succeed in his endeavor. Never had J.J. been so shaken, so moved. In Mr. Robert's teaching he recognized himself as having been a round peg in a square hole. He had transgressed all the laws of success. He had worked strictly for his salary with no concern for the welfare of the company. He now saw the folly of his former attitude and resolved to put his mind and values in proper order.

J.J., now armed with Mr. Robert's guiding wisdom, reflected over his assets and liabilities concerning the workplace and found himself to be sadly lacking in assets. Pondering his likes and dislikes, he realized he must make a career change, but he was unsure about the direction. Discussing it with his wife, he decided to go to evening classes at a local school or college and see what was being offered in adult education.

This proved to be an ideal solution and he promptly enrolled in a subject that had long held his interest. Along with his studies, he surveyed the field of possible employment and targeted a company where he set his heart on working. Now, he began to gather information about the company—its projects and needs. He went to their offices and asked for brochures, which he studied carefully. He went to the company cafeteria and struck up a conversation with an employee in the serving line. They sat together and J.J. learned valuable information that enabled him to better prepare himself to be an asset to the company.

J.J. now invested all his time assuming that he was already a valued employee of the company and in his mind he worked at his job with diligence and great enthusiasm.

One day he knew that the time was right so he called the company and asked the personnel manager for an appointment in the department of his choice.

Now, equipped with precise knowledge, a success attitude, and aware that merit must precede reward, he persuaded the person in charge that his heart was set on working for this particular company; that he felt himself to be a valuable asset to this branch of their operation, and that he expected to be a leader in his field, a winner who would distinguish his department with honor.

J.J. got the job. He had not even mentioned salary, but only that he wanted to prove his conviction that he would enhance and advance the company's purpose.

Thanks to his friend who urged him to attend Mr. Robert's seminar where he received invaluable advice and guidance, J.J. worked his way to the top and is now chairman of the board of one of the country's largest industries. Framed on the wall of his office is the following quotation:

Know what you do, Love what you do, and believe in what you do, And success and money will come and play in your backyard.

— Cavett Robert, Modern Sage;

International Speaker; Founder, National Speakers Association

Fiction

There is no fiction;
imagination is creative.

— **Neville Goddard**

The dictionary defines fiction as "an imaginary statement or story/' and imagination as "existing only in the mind, unreal." But there is not yet a common dictionary definition or description of the natural laws of the mind and how fiction and imagination activate powerful forces in their own likeness.

All that man creates, all progress and enrichment, as well as all that is destructive, is the product of imagination and fiction. It is strictly a matter of cause and effect. There can be no effects without causes, even though the latter may be completely unconscious.

Wherever there is peace, progress and desirable experience, it is the result of repeated imagination. All that is undesirable is created and set in motion by destructive imagination and its habit patterns. The nature and quality of thought is the nature and quality of experience.

An interesting and highly important aspect of fiction is that the creative forces it sets into motion are not necessarily carried out and experienced by the author, although this is most likely. But somewhere a reader, director, performer or someone deeply involved with the storyline, will experience its desirable or undesirable consequences. There is vast evidence of both these results.

Studies have been made of those who are habitually involved with unsavory, sinister or violent themes and their lives have been shown to reflect various conflicts with the natural order of life. Conversely, those who are involved with life- and harmony-promoting themes reflect these elements in their experience.

This book could be filled with the direct and detailed consequences of various fictional disasters, but this is not its purpose. Reference will be made to only one classic and familiar example, that of a book of fiction in which was described in minutest detail the place and circumstances of the sinking of a luxury liner that struck an iceberg in the North Atlantic. Its name and pronunciation could easily have been mistaken for that of the Titanic.

Fiction is a detailed series of images projected upon the impressionable screen of consciousness. There is no inconsequential fiction. Thought sculpts and shapes its likeness into the fibers of our lives.

'Tis strange but true; for truth is always strange; stranger than fiction.

— Lord Byron

Secrets of the Heart

Love conquers all things.
— **Virgil**

Marlaina saw her marriage in seriously troubled waters. What had happened to all the sweetness and caring that had so enriched their lives? Where had the laughter gone, and the playfulness when her husband used to tease her and pick her up and swing her around? Mark no longer did those things; he was a changed man. He had grown selfish, she thought, and insensitive to her needs and pleasures. No, he was not the wonderful man she had married.

Their household was extremely stressed, and their three children reacted to the tense atmosphere in unruly and chaotic behavior. It had become a vicious circle: where would it end? She saw her frustrations in them and knew that their poor performance in school was due to the extreme unhappiness at home.

Both she and Mark were disenchanted with one another, even deeply resentful and she knew that each felt strongly that their love had died as the result of the other's fault.

From Mark's point of view, he spent his life supporting a family from whom he hadn't the least appreciation or consideration. He felt he was taken for granted as a provider and nothing more. He looked for excuses to come home late. There was no pleasure in having dinner with the family. Marlaina only nagged and complained and the children had become unruly brats. Not a pretty sight.

Marlaina knew but chose not to think about the fact that divorce was looming on the horizon. Yes, she was resentful: She had a promising career when they were married, but she had been relegated to a cook, housekeeper, scrubwoman, mistress, shopper, and limousine service. And there was more. She had no time for herself, no way to grow, no sense of reward, consideration or fulfillment. She had been had by life and she was

37

bitter. Mark showed her no affection unless he wanted to make love and then it wasn't love, just a sexual release. Yes, to be sure she had lost all interest in the bedroom.

To Mark, Marlaina was no longer the girl he had married. She was unrecognizable. He thought of how eager she had been and how she was more likely the one to initiate their lovemaking. He compared this to their last intimacy, when he was about to enter the gates of paradise she announced matter of factly, "You forgot to drop your suits off at the cleaners." With these distracting words, Mark had removed himself to the den where he had slept for the last six months or more.

One day Mark came home late from the office and tossed a large envelope on the table with the announcement, "We both know this marriage is on the rocks. I've had our attorney draw up the divorce papers. You will have the house, your car and money for child support. I want out."

Marlaina knew that the marriage was on the rocks but she wasn't prepared for the shock of confronting it face-to-face. What would happen to the children? What and how could she tell them? How would they react to such a tearing and traumatic separation?

Wouldn't they blame her? If not now, then surely later on. Undoubtedly, they would suffer the most. That was the usual scenario, was it not? She felt traumatized. She couldn't speak.

Each felt let down. Their marriage vows had not been honored. And each was convinced that the blame lay at the feet of his partner. Both suffered but there was no communication and their emotions continued to erode.

Every evening Mark asked if she had signed the divorce papers. Marlaina, experiencing shock, resentment and bitterness, remained silent. She could not bring herself even to open the envelope. Bad as things were, she felt that a divorce would be even more intolerable.

One mid-morning Mark called to say that the attorney had gotten a court date for a hearing and asked her to sign the papers as this was delaying the formalities.

The next morning as he was leaving he asked for the signed document. She was too confused to answer. The days wore on with no communication between them. It was all too painful; their beautiful dream had become a nightmare. What could be more dead than a love which had died?

There was no affection in the home. The children became more and more unruly as the stresses in the home mounted. Now there were notes from their teachers that nine-year-old Malinda and seven-year-old Roger were disturbing their classes and were not studying. Would she come to the school and meet with the teachers and the principal? Marlaina went, but matters became worse instead of better. She didn't know where to turn and she was too embarrassed to tell their friends. She sat on the couch in a stupor. She had no appetite and felt weak and haggard.

Mark had constant indigestion and kept popping pills in hope of relief. Never, never again, he thought, if ever he got out of this marriage trap, would he consider losing his freedom for the heavy encumbrances of a family. He thought of the lightness and unobstructed freedom that he had enjoyed before saddling himself with the heavy responsibilities of a family. Why had he not waited? He should have lived more before settling down. Now, his feet were as lead, he was tied and bound for at least another fifteen years when little Roger, now seven, would be in college. He wondered how many men were in the same situation and saw no way out but divorce, although he knew that this would not really resolve the problem. There was the matter of dividing their community property, the problem of financing two homes, visitation rights, and the complications of possible estrangement from the two children. The marriage structure must be changed, he thought, it does not answer the needs of the individual members, and the stresses are too high. Who could survive it?

A month had passed and still Marlaina had not signed the papers. Mark no longer came home for dinner. He hardly saw the children as they were in bed when he returned home. He might have a glimpse of them in the morning, but there was no contact, no warmth. He loved his children and was torn between living in the present misery and living apart from them. How could such a dilemma be resolved?

One morning as Mark left the house, Marlaina turned on the T.V. to distract her confused emotions. On Channel 9 at 7:30 A.M. a program called "There Is A Way" was just starting. The title caused her to linger. Dr. Dale Batesole of Palm Springs introduced a guest who spoke about creating sound relationships. How she hoped there might be some answer to her problem.

She listened for the half-hour but at the end she was in such turmoil that she could not recall what was said. Yet she felt a bit of relief. She then became a regular viewer and day-by-day she gained further clarity as she listened to a different guest five mornings a week. To her, this was a lifesaver. Here she found information and advice that she could use in a very practical sense. From the various guests she began to broaden her perspective and see some of her own responsibility for the chaos in the family. Day-by-day she pieced together the causes of the present conditions and concluded that, either by commission or omission, she had contributed greatly to the family dilemma.

She came to feel that it was the wife who should be the homemaker, especially if she remained in the home, and she saw that she had not acted intelligently in organizing her myriad chores. Trying to muddle through with no order left her no time for herself and she felt relegated to a life of the most boring and wearying enslavement. With this attitude, she could be neither a good wife or mother, and instead of benefiting her family, she had created an untenable atmosphere where everyone was miserable.

She now began to see that she had been unaware of Mark's needs, so busy was she thinking of her own. From the program she learned of the enormous importance of sending a husband off to work in the morning with a bright smile and a hug, to make him feel appreciated and motivated in order to meet the challenges of the day. She saw that she had been greatly remiss in showing no sign of attention when he left in the mornings. She had been too busy complaining about her lot in life to notice that his life was far from a bed of roses, yet she showed him little or no concern.

One day after the program, Marlaina sat contemplating upon what she had heard and thinking of how she could put this into practice in her own life. She drifted into a kind of reverie in which she experienced in imagination a beautiful and ideal life with Mark and their children. She became lost in her vision and was unaware that it endured for over an hour. Most importantly, she felt a wonderful lightness in her mind and heart. Her mind was much clearer and she felt so benefited by her unwitting adventure into the ideal that she resolved to continue the practice daily. At the end of a week she was astonished at the clarity and inner peace that she was feeling after so short a time.

With her new discipline of creative imagination, she now lived in the world of her choice. She saw the children healthy, happy and developing normally. She experienced in the silence of her mind the wonder they used to feel and relived its light and happy moments, its laughter and playfulness. At the end of only two weeks of this new practice she saw reflected in the children an improvement in their behavior: they seemed calmer and less angry.

Mark was still not coming home to dinner and there was no communication between them. Marlaina, recognizing her ignorance in allowing their family life to decline to so devasting a condition, determined that she would restore it to its original health and harmony. She would make every effort to regain Mark's love. She would think only of giving and not at all of getting. She knew that she must empty some of her bitter cup before goodness could refill it.

Without a word to anyone, she set about looking after the children with love and open affection. She bought a book on household

41

organization and learned to so order her life that she now cooked only every other day. She made a week's list of menus at a time and shopped accordingly. Now that she was free most of three days a week, she found she had time to go to the library, to lunch with her friends and enjoy some long-needed leisure.

Though she did not talk with Mark openly, they communicated beautifully in her imaginary conversations. She now cooked the food he liked and served it with soft glances in his direction. He seemed curious as to what had caused the change he observed in her, but was not comfortable to ask.

Within a month of her silent practice, she knew she would win Mark back and renew the harmony in the family. Soon he began to talk to the children in her presence and showed an interest in their lives. Little by little, brief questions or remarks were exchanged between them. He still occupied the den but she detected a slight thawing in his attitude.

The children received their report cards and she noted that their marks were up slightly over the last grading period. She encouraged them and praised them in their father's presence. She noticed how her compliments and affection lifted their spirits and they showed new signs of wanting to please her as well.

She was invited to become an officer in the school PTA, which she cheerfully accepted. The children seemed very pleased that their mother now took an active part in their school. She joined a women's club as well and attended a weekly meeting at the library. Her mind was filled with interesting new growth projects and life again had meaning.

Marlaina suggested to Mark that he might find pleasure in joining some men's club. He looked into the matter and chose one. And he resumed the golf that he had abandoned. Still there had been no open reconciliation between them. But now that each of them had added new interests to their lives there was more to share.

Continuing her daily discipline of creative silent time had completely changed her views and attitudes. She felt and looked as a new person.

She reflected over her seemingly chance discovery of "There Is A Way" and how the engaging Dr. Batesole and his interesting guests had helped her to find her way. She became a faithful and active follower and participant. Though Mark didn't know it, she would tell him one day, that it was this that had brought about the change in her and the priceless benefits to their children. Where once she had been at rock bottom, she now felt that she was close to the top of her climb back to emotional health and happiness.

Encouraged and inspired, she continued to rehearse a variety of scenes and activities which in her mind she and Mark enjoyed together. She practiced greeting him at the door with a cheerful hug and kiss as he left or arrived, asking about his day, offering him some light refreshment. Sitting with him for a cozy chat before dinner, she told him nice or amusing things that the children had said or done, and of her interest and pleasure in her new activities. She imagined that they again enjoyed snuggling in bed together, that there was a bond of tenderness and warmth between them, that they showed open affection before the children. She saw him as the attentive and loving parent that she had recently become.

She knew that her inner practice was showing in her very presence and in all that she did; she was aware that he watched her in silence trying to understand the tremendous change he saw and felt in her. He did not ask and she did not offer any explanation, feeling that deeds were more eloquent than words.

Already a few months had passed and although Mark's response had very noticeably thawed, spring had not yet sprung. But Marlaina was certain that it was just around the corner and would soon be in full bloom. She groomed herself with the meticulous care of their dating days and treated him with warmth, courtesy and grace.

Instead of retreating to his den Mark now sat with the family and watched television or helped the children with their homework. He was not talkative, but he appeared to be more and more comfortable. She knew that he was waiting to see if her new manner would last. She resolved that it would.

One day Mark came home with flowers. He did not offer them to her, but put them in a vase himself and set them on the coffee table. Marlaina remarked that they were beautiful and smiled her pleasure. A couple of weeks later he brought her a book that he said she would enjoy. She soon realized that it was a love story and she knew that he, too, was thinking of the two of them in its happy ending. Still he did not approach her. There had been no touching for almost a year. She chose not to intrude into his emotions but rather to be loving and attentive and allow him to initiate some gesture of desire for her again.

One evening Mark brought home a video cassette of a film that he had seen during their estrangement and put it on the VCR after the children went to bed.

It was a beautiful story with a tender and happy ending which brought tears to Marlaina's eyes. She rose to find a tissue. Mark followed, drawing her to him and holding her firmly and lovingly in his arms. Marlaina's soft weeping erupted into sobs.

So much emotion had passed between them, so many hurts, so much resentment, so many errors in judgment, both stumbling in the darkness of unknowing. He had had no one with whom he felt comfortable to talk, all remained pent up in his disheartened emotions. How painfully both had suffered. Now she knew that it was all self-made.

Mark was as deeply moved; she felt a tear on his cheek as he dried her eyes with his handkerchief. When she could, Marlaina whispered, "Forgive me. Forgive me." And he answered, "Please forgive me too. I knew something was wrong, but I didn't know what it was or what to do about it. Thank God, you brought us back together."

Mark kissed her forehead, her eyelids, her cheeks —and ever so tenderly, her lips. That night, he moved from the den back to their bedroom. Both had learned that love and beauty are the byproducts of selfless giving to others.

Love seems to beautify and inspire all nature.
It raises the earthly caterpillar into the ethereal butterfly,
paints the feathers of spring and lights the glowworm's lamp,
it wakens the song of birds and inspires the poet's lay.

— John Lubbock

The Magic of the Mind

Belief and Assumption

The whole world is hiding in our
thoughts in a seed form.

Baba Hari Dass

It matters little whether our beliefs are factual or entirely false, for belief and assumption are highly creative.

One might rightly ask, how can I practice believing something which my reason and senses would deny? Am I not merely fooling myself?

Not when the natural laws and processes of creation are understood. In order to reinforce it in our mind, it will be repeated throughout this work that our mental thought patterns, beliefs, assumptions, attitudes and emotions are being constantly recorded in our subconscious. And it is the nature and function of this faculty, the subjective and receptive part of our mind, to reflect our mental habits into our outer experience.

Belief in that which our senses do not perceive requires practice. By repetition we come to believe.

While highly useful faculties, as far as they are empowered, reason, logic and the senses are unde-pendable. They are always subject to our degree of knowledge and frame of reference, and our senses can easily mistake one thing for another.

The laws of creation are of a higher order and function dependably when they are activated and sustained, even though we may have little or no conscious awareness of their processes.

Our present circumstances were believed into being, either consciously or unconsciously. Whether we are affluent or financially depressed, favored or unfavored, too heavy or too thin, happy or unhappy, robust or fragile, sick or accident-prone, or consistently in fine fettle, we are expressing our beliefs about ourself, which are stored away in our subconscious programming.

These mental blueprints may date from our earliest childhood. They may have been unconsciously absorbed in our home environment. They could be the effect of a healthy school psychology or its absence, a particular teacher, a sibling at home or someone whose influence was either life-enhancing or destructive.

Happily, we can change the quality of our subconscious programming by the laws of revision. (See that chapter.) Magically, this is not only true of ourselves, but we can do this for others as well. However, we must be very sure that our influence upon others is life- and health-promoting, not only for their well-being, but our own as well. As within, so without.

No great work has ever been accomplished except
by a long interval of musing meditation.

— Walter Bagehot

Unconscious Influences

Solitude, the safeguard of mediocrity, is to genius, the stern friend.

— Ralph Waldo Emerson

Alan K. was in line to become the president of one of the country's giant industries, but he had been passed over two years in a row. It was an important position and paid not only a very substantial annual sum, but offered a yearly bonus as well. Alan was so angry, frustrated and stressed that he began to have the most severe migraine headaches.

Alan had never brought this up at any of the board meetings, thinking that his seniority and outstanding competence would assure his position at the helm; alas, he had guessed wrongly. Now there were jealousies and resentments. And Alan's health was showing the effects. He became more and more stressed and his headaches became intolerable. He asked for a leave of absence to pursue some form of therapy.

In sessions with a career-stress specialist, he recalled an incident in high school that he had long forgotten. Both he and his younger brother had applied for part-time jobs at the school. His brother was accepted for the job he wanted and he was left out. He had never stopped resenting his brother. As college students they were not close and throughout the intervening years they had continued to be estranged.

The specialist helped him to see how unresolved resentment from his early teen years had been undermining his health; all the while its influence had caused invisible fractures in his character and personality. He was told that his migraines were caused at least partially by the unconscious stresses of this unresolved emotion. It was explained that the problem would not go away by ingesting pain medication. It was up to him; no one could do it for him. He must revise the high school incident with his brother in creative imaginal experience to include a happy ending.

49

For several weeks Alan faithfully practiced his revision exercises, and his stresses became noticeably diminished. His headaches were less frequent and less severe. He began to feel a great inner relief—a lightness and new sense of well-being he had not known for many years.

His therapist recommended a fifteen-minute meditation both morning and night to clear the cares of the day and Alan found this to be of enormous benefit. After three months absence, Alan resumed his work free of headaches and free from his unconscious resentments.

He is now the president of his company, he and his estranged brother and their two families are now close. Alan's mental habits have been brought into harmony with the natural order of life.

One of his innovations as president of the company was to establish a stress center where employees could have sessions with a psychologist before minor symptoms became acute, and a child nursery where working mothers could bring their young children and be able to work peacefully knowing that they were well cared for. The two additions paid for themselves in far less absenteeism.

Alan now knows that experience and circumstance are the mirror of the mind and he keeps his thoughts peaceful by his daily "silent time."

It is of the greatest importance that each of us, for even five minutes a day, establish a discipline of stilling our thoughts and allowing our forces to return to free-flowing harmony. Even a week's practice will prove its worth in greater clarity of mind and an increased sense of well being.

Should we feel any resentment, it is wise to forgive, regardless of the circumstances. With this attitude resolution is possible; otherwise trouble compounds. We should become ever more alert to the quality of our thoughts and words. An excellent and effective way is to screen our speech with, "Is it desirable?" If not, there is wisdom in silence.

Where it is a matter of identifying with a negative you must be especially cautious. Expressions such as, "I am tired... exhausted... ill... unhappy... financially depressed... in need," etc., are creating in your life more of the same thing. Whatever the circumstances, these attitudes and expressions will worsen the conditions. They must be eliminated from your mental habits by *replacing them with desirable thoughts.* There is no possibility of improving a situation while concentrating upon the undesirable.

You should be aware that every condition is the effect of a cause, and if you would change the condition you must first change the cause. To think and speak about something undesirable is to energize and create or sustain it. To deny it the energy of our attention and direct our forces toward an ideal solution as though it were already present, weakens the undesirable and strengthens our fulfillment.

Remember that we are enchained to the effects of our mental habits. As our experience is the reflection of our self-programming, we have very little free choice. So we must be cautious about "the quality of our thoughts," for it is the cause of our conditions and circumstances.

Will you join me, dear friend, in screening our thoughts and words with the Mental Guardian, "Is this desirable"? And if not, let us turn at once to the positive, to all that is life, health and harmony enhancing.

Where there is peace and silence there is neither anxiety nor doubt.

—**St. Francis of Assisi**

The Magic of the Mind

Word Power

There is a weird power in a spoken word.

— Joseph Conrad

In keeping with the natural laws of the mind, our dominant thoughts tend to create and sustain their likeness in our experience. We express our ideas and concepts in word symbols, which invoke their vibratory equivalent within our lifeforce field. Thus, our every spoken word is influencing the quality of our lives. One could rightly say that to improve the quality of our vocabulary by expressing thoughts that are life-enhancing is to upgrade the quality of our destiny.

This is far more significant than first meets the eye. To fully understand that thoughts and words are highly creative is the first step in determining the quality of our life.

This has long been known by the sages of the world, as reflected in the biblical statement of Proverbs 18:4: "The words of a man's mouth are deep waters."

All that we think and speak initiates natural forces that interact within our being, either increasing or diminishing the quality of our lives.

It is human nature to desire peace, harmony and fulfillment, and to one of discernment, our choice of word symbols is a clear indication of the state of our mind, our circumstances and our destiny.

Emotion is an important part of the creative process and is largely the conditioned response to familiar conditions. Most of our reactions are automatic, but we can groom them toward that which is desirable and in harmony with life.

The familiar adage, "Unless we can say something nice about someone, we should say nothing at all," is well grounded in natural law,

53

for disdaining undesirable traits in others activates the same energy pattern in our own vibrations. This psychochemical reaction affects our own well-being.

We should guard and groom our choice of words, for according to the wise, they soon disclose our weaknesses or triumphs, our frailties or our greatness.

Colors fade, temples crumble, empires fall, but wise words endure.

— Joseph Conrad

Traditional Roles

Things do not happen in this world; they are brought about.

— Hays

Mary B.'s father had long been in the field of aeronautics and throughout her childhood he had given her toy planes and explained the function of various parts. She had grown up with a passion for this field and chose it as her major in college. Having completed her studies with honors, she also received her master's degree in this field. Excited and eager to enter the work force, she followed her father's advice and proceeded in the proper manner. But to her dismay, and for no reason which she could discern, she had not been engaged by any of the many firms where she had applied. Despairing of ever finding work in her field, she was not only losing her bright spirit and her confidence, but seemed to be going through a whole personality change.

Her father knew that she was better qualified than some of the men who found employment and understood that it was a matter of her trying to break through traditional roles of a strictly male-oriented industry. Mary knew it as well and they had talked of it at times, but he had advised her not to dwell upon the negatives of anything she desired as this tended to make things worse. So she pressed on, pursuing her goal with determined vigor. Yet, there was no change.

Mary was bright, spirited, and very pretty. More often, in her regard, the term used was *beautiful.* She had a pleasant personality and worked well with others. Why could she not get a job?

A new opportunity arose and she went for another interview. This time the personnel manager was a woman and it proceeded a little differently. After learning of her well-above-average credentials, she was asked if she had applied elsewhere and if so, what had been the reaction of the interviewers? Mary explained that everyone had found her qualifications impressive; they often kept her at length and seemed genuinely interested in employing her, yet nothing ever came of it. She asked for an explanation.

To Mary's surprise, she heard the last thing she could have expected. She knew that hers had long been a man's field and that men might resist setting a precedent—opening the doors to women could jeopardize their jobs. But she was not prepared to hear that her problem was that of being too beautiful. Her figure, she was told, would disrupt the whole department. Men would be watching her willowy hips and sweater model bust-line instead of their work. The lady had added, "Instead of an asset, you would be a liability to the company—even a disaster. No one in their right mind is going to take the responsibility for putting a lamb in with the wolves. Oh, they're all great fellows, but you must understand that a beautiful young woman would distract the men from their work. I'm sorry, but I see no way to consider your application."

Mary's heart sank, and she was about to rise and leave when it occurred to her that she could make herself less attractive by the way she dressed and groomed herself. So she asked not to be taken out of the file of possible candidates and requested another brief appointment two weeks hence. The lady felt that she had made up her mind, but Mary was so warm and personable that she agreed and noted it among her appointments.

Mary had a plan: she would wear a loose pants-suit that did not flatter her figure. She would wear no make-up and flatten her hair back into a short pony tail. And she would wear unnecessary heavy, black-rimmed glasses, to further make herself as invisible as possible. She was sure this would work.

For the following two weeks, Mary practiced imaginary scenes and conversations confirming her employment with the company. In her mind she praised the work of her colleagues. She asked their advice and showed warm appreciation for their help. She found ways of being useful to them and established a friendly but professional working relationship.

So completely did she think of her efforts as being a highly effective asset to the company that she gave no thought to her salary.

To her delight, she had recovered her spirit by giving of her efforts for the benefit of all concerned. When she kept her appointment with the personnel manager, she was met with, "My word! You are unrecognizable. Most women dress up to look better; this is the first time I've seen one dress down to look worse.

'I'll take a chance with you," she added, "but if there are any complaints about your being a liability to the department, you'll have to move on."

As the result of her self-programming of being already happily employed, and in her fantasies doing that which she would be doing were it already realized, she transcended the negative energy currents and vibrated in a higher orbit.

Mary has now been with the company as a valued employee for almost seven years, is highly motivated and much appreciated by her colleagues.

In retrospect, she saw that she should have done her preparatory work in "creative imagination" before her very first interview. She should have rehearsed its consequent activity "in the ideal" before ever making an appointment. She now knew that had she done so, she would have been working long before she succeeded in getting her first job.

With this valuable lesson, Mary has since used the creative laws of the mind in all her projects and has become remarkably proficient in all she undertakes. She shares this knowledge with others and reminds them of the importance of "the laws of assumption"— that by assuming our desire to be already realized, then doing in the silence of our mind that which would naturally follow, we actually create the condition. In other words we have initiated the cause which sets the effect into motion. Mary also learned that no matter how traditional something may be, that the repetition of creative thought patterns can transcend and transmute established patterns.

Every man's destiny is in his own hands.

— Sidney Smith

The Pairs of Opposites

Balance is the thing to strive for.

— William Ross

In observing the creative nature and processes of the mind we find that all manifest existence and experience derive from the interplay of equal but opposite forces. Mind is the architect, imagination, the process and the pairs of opposites, the building blocks.

Normally, we think of opposites as entirely separate and removed from one another. Actually, they are inseparably united and vary only in degree. Hot and cold, up and down, happy and sad, love and hate, rich and poor, comfort and pain, young and old, health and sickness—each of these represents interacting forces that are unconsciously activated by our thoughts, attitudes and self-image. The degree to which they are experienced is determined by our state of equilibrium and centeredness. To be in harmony with life we must be balanced between the pairs of opposites.

At first glance we would assume that we should identify with the positive end of the pole—happiness instead of sadness, comfort instead of pain, wealth instead of poverty, etc.; yet this is not being centered. To concentrate solely on happiness would be off-center, and life in its natural flow would re-establish its balance. Happiness should be a by-product, not an end in itself. One cannot remain in an ultimate state of joy and excitement; it would be out of synch. The degree of the rise above the line of equilibrium is the degree of the fall below. Such an effort could only result in peaks and valleys. There is no healthy peace of mind at either extreme. To be in harmony with the natural laws, we must groom our thoughts to flow easily and smoothly through life. The main highway is through the center of the pairs of opposites.

Centeredness is a place of beauty where a sense of well-being underlies all that we feel and do. We feel good about ourselves and reflect this to others. Our thoughts smooth and prepare the way.

How do we approach and establish this centering between the opposite poles? Throughout untold centuries, the best way has been found to be that of a daily habit of at least a few minutes of "silent time." Many executives and people of great responsibility now close their office doors and ask not to be disturbed for a specified time while they focus their attention upon a quiet and lovely scene in the country, or imagine that they are lying on the grass under a beautiful shade tree, or perhaps counting their breath up to five and back again. Some keep soft and soothing music playing in their offices and in their cars when they drive. The benefits of staying in balance and flowing with the tides of life are beyond measure.

Everyone is attracted to beauty, whether it be in nature, a person or the broad field of art. Beauty is harmony, balance, equilibrium—that which speaks to the subtleties of the soul. It is the center path between the pairs of opposites.

The same laws obtain throughout all manifest existence. It is the balance, the equilibrium between these two forces that sustains the planets in their orbits, the galaxies in their positions and every infinitesimal fragment in its place in the great cosmic procession.

Though the eye cannot perceive it and its complexity dazzles the mind, the sciences of the great and the small are finding in the orchestrated rhythms of the infinite, a factual phenomenon long called "The Music of the Spheres," and the choreography of the all-pervading dance of the celestial parade.

Yet it is true that nature's source and purpose are an unfathomable mystery to human intelligence, for the answers lie in frequencies far transcending the capacity of the intellect. Still, to the relatively few great contemplatives of the highest order, these mysteries have been known in their fullness since ages lost in antiquity.

If not by means of the intellect, how was this elusive knowledge acquired? By using the mind to transcend itself. There are disciplines by which it can be freed from its limited and enchaining frequencies and rise into those higher dimensions of "direct knowing."

Consciously or not, we are all seeking harmony, for this is the only state that is truly and lastingly comfortable. Yet, who does not become ruffled and out of sorts at times? This is understood; everyone has imperfections, but an effective way to restore your harmony is to take a few minutes, sit quietly alone, and visualize a poetically beautiful little lake, sur-rounded by the loveliest graceful trees and soft green grass.

We might step into the scene, glance about, then sit down comfortably on nature's velvety carpet just above the water line. There is not a leaf stirring, not a ripple on the lake. The water is pure and crystal clear. You can see into its depths. It is at rest. It is in perfect harmony. And you have allowed the quiet and subtle beauty and stillness to restore your harmony.

You are at peace through and through, and you will sustain and reflect in your eyes and face, your every glance and motion, the pure beauty of your spirit. You are your own wonderful self again. And each time it is practiced it becomes more beneficial, for it restores your peaceful balance.

You are now experiencing the wonder, the nobility and the serenity of your gentle nature, balanced midway between the pairs of opposites.

A well-balanced person never does any single thing to the exclusion of everything else. He has learned that the enjoyment of anything is lost just the moment he gets too much of that thing. He quits eating just before he becomes completely satisfied. Watches constantly his balance or poise.

There are so few people in the world possessing this rare quality that the ones who have it shine like stars.

— A. B. Zutavern

Marriage and the Creative Process

The ideal marriage is not one in which two people marry to be happy, but to make each other happy.

— Roy L. Smith

Two young couples, the closest of friends since high school, were planning a double wedding. But in view of the high divorce rate, they decided to make a study of the reasons for failure, and to explore the means of reducing the risk factor. It was agreed that each of the four would utilize the library, coordinate their reading and meet once a week for dinner at their alternate apartments to share what they had learned.

In their first session, the notes of one member revealed that love is blinding to those who have not yet experienced all the mounting difficulties and hardships of raising a family. All couples appear to believe that their devotion will surmount any and all problems that could arise, that their love will endure forever in its same beauty, and that in reaching their autumn years they will walk happily into the sunset. Studies show that no amount of advice can convince either party that these beautiful visions are all too seldom realized, and that a great challenge lay ahead. The two young couples recognized themselves in this scenario.

From the notes of another they learned that lack of information and inadequate preparation were the principal causes of disenchantment following the honeymoon. The study pointed out that there is rarely a saint and a villain, but rather both parties contributing to the erosion of the relationship.

A third member read a long list of the basic problems particular to marriage that result in great suffering for all members of the family and which few couples either avoid or resolve. The report gave the basic reasons for marriage as that of protection for the expectant mother, the care of the young and the assurance of both role models in their upbringing. These principles seemed basic, valid and worthy; why were they not working? Why were they so difficult to implement?

The study of the fourth member disclosed that the problems resulting in a growing epidemic of divorce and its devastating consequences are less the fault of both well-intentioned partners than that of the heavy responsibilities and hardships imposed by the marriage structure itself.

Each of the four was astonished and dismayed at the seemingly insurmountable obstacles that most couples encounter. How and why, they all wondered, was something so beautiful and full of promise the source of centuries-old satirical jokes, outright contempt, and with sarcasm referred to as the "marriage-trap?"

Realizing that without serious study and preparation, the beauty of their dreams could change into nightmares, they delayed their marriages in favor of further study and better planning. This concerted effort became their first priority and occupied all their free time. They devoured books and shared their learning. They attended lectures and studied statistical surveys.

Further research revealed that moral values and acceptable behavior were greatly a matter of geography and tradition. In some countries, the age-old custom of multiple wives is still approved and sanctioned by both religion and state. And it was clear that sound and practical reasons underlay this tradition. One, immediately obvious, was the smaller number of men due to the perils of survival in the wilderness of the times. Conflict and war often took a heavy toll on the male population.

With the conditions of earlier ages, a woman unprotected and unprovided for by a male was unlikely to survive. So necessity dictated that the fewer men should protect and provide for several wives.

In their effort toward a broader view of the human equation, the two couples learned that morality arose, in the main, from circumstance and was as varied as the many countries and their myriad traditions.

They learned that inhabitants of the northernmost regions of the earth had practiced an age-old custom of welcoming a far distant traveler who had survived the perils of blinding and freezing snowstorms, the hungry polar bear or avalanche by honoring him with food, shelter and the favors of his wife.

Clearly, that which was moral could be dictated by life-threatening conditions. The wisdom of nature had set the precedent throughout the earth, by adapting morality to circumstance and need.

The studies of the four young marriage candidates expanded their awareness to the millions of years when developing man had been strictly a hunter and gatherer—dominant, free, brave and adventurous. This was a far longer period than the few thousand years of the evolving nuclear family. Still lingering in his genes, they learned, are the encoded memories of the freedom of his past, and his need to express his manliness, his superior strength and prowess. This is clearly evident in his attraction to the daring sports of boxing, wrestling, football, racing, sky-diving, circus and rodeo feats, the martial arts and similar pursuits.

They saw that the tightly structured and confining role imposed upon the male by modern society enchains his expression of those natural aspects of his nature for which he is still greatly admired: bravery, competitive feats, resourcefulness, protection, adventure and strength.

They learned that the changing role of men and the demands made upon them appear to be even greater stresses than those of modern women, who outlive men by several years. And that society at large, while becoming more aware of the longstanding hardships of women, seems relatively unaware of the painful lot of men and the stresses upon their spirit and health.

Further study expanded their awareness of the changing role of women, mainly during this century, and their need to develop their minds and express themselves outside the home. They discussed the problem of combining child rearing with a career while still serving the entire family.

Birth control had given women a measure of freedom, but the major issues were yet to be resolved. Happy housewives were few indeed.

In matters of children, authorities advised that physical punishment was primitive, psychically harmful and inadmissable. A calm and quiet explanation and the denial of privileges is more effective.

The parent's actions must be worthy of respect and invoke a sense of justice in the child's eyes. One member read that children's questions about their origin should be answered honestly, if sparingly, and that a child needs to learn that what he is taught is true and dependable. He will not have the same confidence in his source of knowledge when he learns that babies are not brought by the stork, or as in France, found in a cabbage. When this information is begun before the age of embarrassment it can be added to as the child's curiosity develops. A well-informed child is far more likely to make the right judgment and avoid the often devastating consequences.

Two of the most common false teachings that have contributed to the suffering and ruin of untold thousands of marriages, they learned, are well-intentioned, but misinterpretations. One is believing the nude body to be vulgar, indecent and to be hidden at all costs; the other is the ignorant notion that lovemaking is sinful and therefore all babies are born in sin. This is due to the inability to discern in the literal word of the Bible the mystical wisdom it conceals.

In their wide reading they found that books by marriage counselors were an excellent source for solutions to the classic problems most couples confront. So, our four marriage candidates, recognizing the folly of entering into the most complex of relationships with no instruction and preparation, decided to find a highly qualified marriage counselor with whom they would each have a private session once a month on a continuing basis. This would provide the foresight, planning and organization that must be the foundation of any successful endeavor.

After making a survey of the marriage counselors in their area, they prepared a list of names and one in their group called each with initial questions. Noting the answers from each call, the four friends discussed this information, which included the educational background, degrees—if any, their years of professional counseling, their marital and parental status, whether or not an organized program was offered, and if they had done any teaching or writing on the subject. Lastly, terms for the monthly service for each of the four were discussed.

It was decided to choose the three most interesting from the list and make an appointment with each for the two couples together. Afterward, they would evaluate their impressions and select the counselor who was most appealing to the four. This proved highly interesting and they established themselves with a very wise lady and began their sessions together. They were given progressive reading material and a guidelines debit and credit ledger. All were delighted with the informative and mind-stretching program and followed it joyfully and meticulously. After a few months of fundamental preparation, their counselor suggested that they were ready to set their double wedding date. Following the ceremony, the two happy and much wiser couples left for a week's honeymoon cruise.

And here we shall leave them in the wise shepherding of their counselor, and return some years hence to see how their training and its application has affected their lives.

An author friend of their counselor, writing a book on compatibility in marriage, asked to meet with them for research purposes. The four agreed and he found them discussing the following excerpts from Shakespeare:

> Neither a borrower nor a lender be,
> For loan oft loses both itself and friend.
> Have more than thou showest,
> Speak less than thou knowest,
> Lend less than thou owest.

One of the wives quoted William James's discerning insight: 'The art of being wise is the art of--knowing what to overlook." "Indeed!" agreed the — author, then shortly asked for the single most beneficial aspect of their marriage guidelines training.

All four enthusiastically concurred that it was the daily record keeping in their debit and credit ledgers, together with their monthly sessions with their counselor. This enabled them to review and evaluate their daily performance, and it was studied in their monthly counseling sessions. Hearing all the concerns of each partner enabled the counselor to steer them clear of the classic pitfalls.

Questioning about their families revealed that one couple had two children, the other, three. All the offspring were healthy, happy, respectful, and courteous good students who enjoyed mutual affection with their parents.

The two families were the closest of friends and a valued support group for one another. Their comfortable homes were within a few minutes drive of each other and they socialized frequently. Each couple enjoyed other friends as well and the benefits of their counselor's training were passed among them.

Asked for further details, one of the wives said that the counselor's organization program had provided for each mother to keep the child or children of the other for one full day a week to enable her to use this time as she chose. They often exchanged weekend care so the parents could enjoy free time together. They divided their two-week vacations into one week every six months and kept each other's children, who were beloved by both couples.

Questioned as to continuing with their counselor, the four responded, "absolutely," as the major credit for their still-happy marriages after fourteen years was truly hers.

The author, still curious about the ledger, asked how they self-evaluated their performance as a partner. A daily entry was made, they explained, with 100% for excellence, 50% for average, and lesser credits for poor performance. No attention to the requirement rightly received a zero. Demerits also had their value ratings and at the end of the day, each partner reviewed his debits and credits, added the column and had a clear picture of his performance. In the passing weeks and months he was able to see the state of his marriage. At their monthly sessions, their counselor evaluated the ledger and made suggestions accordingly.

Wisely guided in all the major aspects of their lives, the greatest emphasis was placed upon the continuation of the behavior of both parties as it had been during the honeymoon. Recognizing the difficulty of sustaining the same attentive and tender habits after the responsibility of children and mounting hardships, their counselor played an enormously important role during those early years.

The most important single aspect of their training was that of placing their partner's happiness and well-being before their own. Every day, each was to give some attention to that which would please his partner, and it was the duty of the spouse to respond to this kindness with sincere and cheerful appreciation. Another accent was upon attentive listening to one another's needs and comments, and responding satisfactorily.

It was pointed out that if one partner's needs were being met while the other felt unfulfilled, this was a serious alarm that required immediate attention. Even twenty-four hours delay in restoring harmony would allow for erosion of the marriage to begin. Small though it may be, unless feelings are restored to inner peace and harmony, a minor resentment left unresolved will likely go the way of one bad apple spoiling the lot.

High on the list of their training was mutual courtesy and daily, outspoken appreciation. Each was to expressly look for and comment on the other's virtues and kindly deeds. They were also encouraged to do so in the presence of their children and friends, and apply it to them as well.

Among their various guidelines was attention to organization and timing, contributing greatly to the smooth and easy flow of relationships. This alone, eliminates stress.

Another important factor was that of preparing meals in a bright and cheerful atmosphere, happy mealtime being basic to the health of a family. The wives learned to cook only every other day, and later on the children were taught to help.

Their counselor insisted upon open and demonstrative affection between all members of the family, and this was to be visible at least every morning and evening. Children were to be praised and hugged for every sign of service, kindness and pleasant behavior. Everyone was expected to try to bring out the best in one another; to look for the positive and to be quick with cheerful praise.

Special attention was given to selected soft music that was always played at mealtime on auto-reverse cassettes. Music was enjoyed at home during most of their waking hours and set a pleasant and relaxed mood.

Careful attention was also given to color in the home as well as in their clothing, as it invokes unconscious responses. All was in soft, clear and harmonious tones. Color harmony was carried out on the table and even in the food.

Their counselor had advised them that instruction on natural functions of the body should be taught to their children beginning around four-to-five years of age, well before the teen years when embarrassment would cause rejection. Meanwhile, the children's accumulating knowledge was built upon solid ground, and on reaching their teens they were already well-informed and able to make sound judgments.

Recognizing its enormous importance, the two couples established a daily discipline of responding to a one-page review of their guidelines, which kept right thought and right action in the forefront of their minds. "You can only 'win' with this system," they assured the author.

When asked how long they had used this method, they answered "fourteen years" —more than adequate proof of its validity. Both couples and their children were healthy, happy and entirely pleased with the direction of their lives.

Pressed for other details of their guidelines program, they said that table habits, bathroom habits and bedroom habits were high on their list for special attention. Mealtime must become imprinted in the subconscious as a happy togetherness and sharing time. This establishes a vitally important free-flowing harmony throughout the body's interacting systems. Bathroom habits were a matter of neatness and order. Bedtime was drawing to a close all the day's activity, settling down—a time for affection before sleep. With parents and children together, the young should be held quietly and lovingly by both parents and given full attention. This should not be a quick peck on the cheek or forehead, but at least several minutes of quiet togetherness as a family. Affectionate signs of approval are magical to children of all ages as they prepare to sleep. Young adults in residence are no exception. Practiced together in each other's presence, the family unit will develop deep and loving lifetime roots, and add stability to the lives of each member.

And the bedroom habits of the parents, are they included in the guidelines? The author asked. Yes, in their training this was the most fragile and crucial area of human relationships, and one of the richest and most rewarding if wisely attended to. All aspects of behavior in this area should be groomed to promote harmony.

The couples discovered that sleeping in the nude has both positive and negative elements. Psychologically, the positives appear to be outweighed by the negatives. If the senses become accustomed to nudity, it is less stimulating than when kept for tender moments. Except for nudists, who have their own values, an unattractive nude body should not be paraded about nor displayed in casual sitting or reclining. A semblance of covering is more aesthetically appealing.

Both families taught their children that the nude body was neither vulgar nor indecent, that attire is a matter of appropriateness. A nude baby on the beach, around a well-enclosed yard for safety, or a supervised splash pool can be charming; but older mixed sexes should be slightly clothed. The counselor explained that teaching little girls that their nude body was shameful resulted in untold thousands of ruined marriages with countless frigid wives. She advised that, except for nudists, parents should not be nude around the home; neither should there be any scrambling for cover when surprised by the presence of a child. This is an alarming sign that there is something "bad" about one's natural self.

From many years of listening to couples' complaints, fears and desires, the counselor developed the following guidelines for intimacy in the bedroom:

If pleasures and closeness are to endure, love-making should be made its most romantic and beautiful.

The first order of concern is to keep the pleasure of one's partner before one's own.

The second, is to engage only in that which is mutually pleasurable. One's likes and dislikes should be delicately discussed, keeping in mind that love and its expression is as a delicate and fragile flower, enhanced by caring sweetness, but destroyed by insensitivity.

It should be understood that the sexual nature of men and women are wisely different, due to their respective physiology and roles. Women need more open and demonstrative affection not only in the bedroom but in general. If her interest in intimacy is to endure, affection should be a daily expression of both parties.

Men should be aware that most women need at least a few minutes of mutually tender touching and caressing before they are ready for union. The love-making embrace should always begin with affection in the northern hemisphere, beginning with tender kisses and caresses, then warming to more pronounced desire. Attention should then move southward to the softness of the twin cushions of sensual delight where unhurried caressing will be richly rewarded in the cooperation of the female. With signs of her mounting response, he should proceed caressingly to the southern hemisphere. And if he is wise, he will find it magical to her pleasure to linger and explore the miniature crest above the mysterious inner passage.

Reciprocally, a woman's first order of concern is to remember that his pleasure must be her single purpose. Men, contrary to what some women believe, need the same tender caressing of their corresponding parts as foreplay to lovemaking. Mounting desire will guide a woman in fondling his most sensitive areas. Her gift of love in this magnetic terrain will dazzle her mind, senses and emotions.

Women, or men, who feel inhibited about pleasuring their mates can familiarize themselves on a gradual basis by using the creative process to imagine themselves bestowing such pleasure and the resulting delight of their partner. Overcoming initial aversions, many women and men learn to enjoy such sensual giving and joyfully add it to their repertoire of love-making.

Penetration should only occur when all physical signs are present and the woman is intensely eager and sweetly aggressive. From here, wise nature will guide both partners to ecstasy.

All of this advice, and more, our happy couples employed in the service of their marriages. Their wise counselor knew of the benefits of the creative process of the mind and continually reminded them to hold their marriages in the ideal, resolving any lapses in communication with an openness to the positive qualities of their spouse. Both couples continue with their counselor and give her full credit for their ideal and enriching family life.

The basic needs for a successful marriage? That leaves, it seems to me, but one recourse: a purposeful, willing, sympathetic desire on the part of the male and female to understand each other. Such understanding presupposes a willingness to give as well as to take, to forget as well as to remember; to love as well as to be loved; to become mature rather than remain infantile in our reactions to the people in our immediate environment.

— **Peter Steincrohn, M.D.**

Reason and Logic

I will not reason and compare. My business is to create.

— William Blake

In the hierarchy of human faculties, reason and logic hold highly esteemed offices. Their function is that of ministries of the mind. Not unlike our other faculties, they too, have their subordinate officers with their different departments.

In their own domain, they are highly valid and we would be hard pressed to function without them; but it should be remembered that reason and logic are only as sound as the extent of our knowledge. As knowledge expands and widens, reason must be revised.

All too often we allow it to block our path to higher achievement. We reason that our desire requires finances well beyond our means, that we are too young, too old, too early, too late or the myriad other excuses born of our limited knowledge and reason. Nothing has delayed our progress and fulfillment as much as our limited reasoning.

In making our judgment, there should be only two considerations: Is the desire possible to the natural order of life, and will it benefit everyone whom it affects? If the latter is affirmative, then reason should be bypassed in favor of "acceptance." We have a green light and there are no obstacles on our path except those we create.

How can we be certain that our desire is within the harmony of the natural order of life? Here, reason is invaluable; it tells us that it is untimely to begin a career in ballet in our autumn years, or to attempt to teach philosophy before reaching our teens. It reminds us that all manifest existence has its own natural progression, and is consistent and dependable. — All too often the question of "how to" closes all doors before us. The phrase "how can I?" is out of place when we have clarified the two considerations: Is it possible and is it morally justified? The ways and means are not our concern if we proceed by the natural laws of the mind, for the mind has means of which we are unaware.

So long as you are concerned with by means of,
you will always be depending on something else.

— Huang Po Ancient Chinese Sage

The College Student

It is not in the stars to hold our destiny, but in ourselves.

— William Shakespeare

Tom was failing in college, especially in math, which was his weakest subject. It was at least partially due to the fact that his modest means required his working nights to pay the ever-rising tuition, his rent and food. He was always sleepy when he tried to study and the noise and disturbance was so discouraging that he was considering dropping out, getting a day job and relieving his stresses. Still, Tom hated facing the future with no expertise and being relegated to the leftovers of life. He despaired of ever graduating or resolving his dilemma.

One night, a diner in the all night restaurant where Tom worked as a waiter, forgot a book on his table. Tom noticed that it was entitled *Imagination* and in the wee hours when things were quiet he began to browse through its pages. The author described the function of the mind and how to initiate the right causes for the desired effect. So fascinated was Tom that he took the book home, devoured it, and returned it to the restaurant the following evening. He felt that the instruction held the solution to his problem and he set about putting it into practice.

Though it seemed to him highly speculative, Tom changed his attitude from worry to creative imagination by assuming that he had already graduated and was now enjoying the consequences. After about a week's practice he discovered that he could determine his own state of mind. Where he had been discouraged, he was now creating his self-designed future and already felt lighter and brighter.

With a postive attitude Tom practiced thinking that he had a great job. Shortly he was motivated to cross the campus to the office of employment to see if there was anything new. Noticing a listing with that day's date, he found that it was a request for a live-in babysitter. He hadn't thought of himself in such a role but decided to check it out. To his great surprise, the request came from the home of an astrophysics professor. The duties were very light and it offered a pleasant room, food and a bit of pocket money. Realizing that this was infinitely better than his present situation, Tom jumped at the chance.

The couple was pleasant, and watching the baby while they were frequently out was an ideal time for him to study.

About twice a month the couple invited friends to dinner and Tom enjoyed helping his working hostess prepare and serve the food. He was so pleased to live in their pleasant home and to be treated with kindness and respect, he looked for ways to help them well beyond their expectations. To show his appreciation and growing affection for his hosts and their child, he elected to do all the cleaning, shopping, errands, and help the professor with his home preparations for class, as well as look after the child.

His host, a brilliant and resourceful professor, suggested that Tom prepare for a teaching career at the university level. Tom felt that he had not had sufficient preparation in math, so essential to that field, although he was fascinated by the subject. The professor offered to teach him all that was required to prepare him for this prestigious position. Tom couldn't believe his good fortune. His spirits soared. With his less than modest means and inadequate preparation, he could never have hoped for such a marvelous career.

How, he wondered, could he have been so lucky? But on reflection, he realized that it had not been luck, but his desire to improve his conditions and his effort to check out offers of employment on the campus bulletin board. Yet, the fact that he was engaged to take care of the child, with light home duties, did not account for this most incredible career opportunity; to be privately tutored by so respected a person was an honor for which he could find no merit.

Tom was beside himself with joy. With the help of the professor, he was assured not only of graduating, but of becoming a full-fledged professor of one of the most highly advanced sciences. His elation mounted, his love and appreciation for both his hosts and their dear child were unbounded, and the spring in his step was so light that he could barely feel the ground under his feet.

With the help of his professor, Tom made great strides in his studies. And the mutual benefits of their home arrangement were so delightful and highly valued by all that Tom remained in the family throughout his studies, his graduation and the additional degrees required for his teaching career. Best of all, his host was instrumental in his receiving a professorship at his alma mater.

One day Tom asked his host why, with no merit on his part, he had offered him the honor of his private coaching to prepare him for his career. He was astonished and deeply moved by the unexpected answer he received. "Because," said his host, "you gave your best effort to all you undertook. Your attention to our comfort and pleasure has been unbounded, and you are persevering and meticulous in all details. Together with your natural intelligence, this is the stuff of which able physicists are made." Tom turned his head away to conceal his misty eyes.

It takes a person who is wide awake to make his dreams come true.

— Roger Bacon

The Magic of the Mind

80

Dinner for Twelve

Success in life is a matter not so much of talent or opportunity,
as of concentration and perseverance.

— C W. Wendte

Mr. and Mrs. C. wanted to buy a home in Pacific Palisades, overlooking the ocean near Los Angeles, and Mr. C. gave his wife a figure beyond which he was unwilling to pay. Driving around the area where they wanted to live, she searched amongst the many handsome homes for one with a "For Sale" sign which would meet their requirements.

Her vision was clearly detailed: She wanted four or five bedrooms with as many baths, a large living room and large separate dining room, another sitting room for game tables, television and wetbar. In addition, she wanted a large front and back garden with trees and flowers, a bright roomy kitchen, butler's pantry, service porch, laundry room, maid's quarters, at least a three-car garage and ample guest parking. But most of all, she wanted all the rooms to have an ocean view. Her husband thought her long list of specifications was surely nonexistent. In no way, he thought, would she ever find already built such a precisely self-designed house.

Several times Mrs. C. passed by what appeared to be just such a house except that she felt it unlikely that all the rooms had an ocean view; she did not ask to see its interior.

One day, passing the house with a friend, she pointed it out and remarked what a pity that it was surely missing the ocean view that was so important to her. Her friend disagreed, felt that most of the rooms would have such a view, and she urged Mrs. C. to ask to be shown the house. Upon seeing it, she and her husband both fell in love with it at once and felt that it was truly "their house." But when they were told the price, Mr. C. found it greatly exaggerated and refused even to consider

81

the purchase. In fact, he left the following day for business affairs in the East, and told his wife to forget that house and look for another within the price range he had specified.

But Mrs. C. had already imprinted in her subconscious a house with its precise features, and she knew that this was equivalent to finding the proverbial needle in the haystack. She was not ready to abandon her dream so quickly. But, respecting and adoring her husband, neither would she disturb his peace of mind. He had made a generous offer and it was rejected; she could not ask more of him. So she drove him to the airport and said a smiling and loving goodbye. Now she knew that "if it's to be, it's up to me," and as she drove back home she made a decision: She would mentally live in that house and practice believing that all parties concerned were happy with the outcome.

Having young children and the many distractions of family life, she felt the need to be mostly alone in order to concentrate on her project. Instructing her housekeeper that except for meals with the children and at their bedtime she did not wish to be disturbed, Mrs. C. stayed in bed for three days and nights. She had never confronted such an impasse and knew of no other way to sustain her focused attention on "living in the house." She knew that it would require all her creative forces if she were to break the spell and reverse the seemingly impossible deadlock.

Not knowing quite how to go about it, her thoughts ranged over a suitable plan. At last, it occurred to her to give a dinner party in the new house. She would invite several friends who would be especially happy about the purchase, and it would be an evening of joy and delight.

In her creative imagination, all the family activity occurred in that house. From there she planned the dinner party, invited the guests and composed the dialogue of their bright conversations. Gathering flowers from the garden she made several large floral arrangements to enhance its beauty. Again and again she rehearsed every aspect of the evening. Repeatedly she heard her husband express his pleasure over the mutually satisfying agreement. Including their two young sons of ten and twelve in the celebration of their new home, she rehearsed them as always in the proper behavior of dining with adults, coaching each one with a funny story that he could tell at the table when she gave the signal.

During all her waking hours Mrs. C. remained concentrated upon some aspect of their happy life in their new home. When she joined her sons for meals and at their bedtime she pretended that it was all occurring in her dream house. And when she went to bed she lay her head on the pillow in the lovely bedroom of the new home and thought of her actual location in its relative direction.

After three days of concentration in her bedroom she resumed her usual habits with the children, but sustained her inner vision. As she drove about in the car she practiced feeling that she was leaving and returning to the new place. It was the foundation upon which all else occurred.

Several days later her husband returned from the East Coast and asked if she had found another house. Answering no, she showed no emotion and turned to something else, but continued to experience its realization.

Within the week the impasse resolved itself, and one month later Mrs. C, radiant with joy, gave her dinner for twelve in the house of her dreams.

There is a key to every door. That key is persistence.

— A. B. Zutavern

Mental Blueprint

Your life will be no better than the plans you make
and the actions you take.

— A. A. Montapert

The family doctor advised Mr. and Mrs. B. that the Southern California climate near the ocean would greatly benefit the health of the elder of their two young sons. So, it was decided that the couple would soon fly out to the West Coast to look into the project. They hoped to find a suitable rental for a year while deciding upon a house to buy.

During the month before leaving, Mrs. B. rehearsed a nightly scene in which she imagined that she was in California and that the East Coast was far away. In her creative fantasies she experienced the family as settled into a charming house on a street corner with lots of tall trees, and enormous windows everywhere. She saw and experienced the four of them swimming in the lovely garden pool surrounded with flowering plants. In her mind she looked out upon the blue Pacific and walked with the family down to swim in the ocean as well. She saw their elder son in vigorous and robust health and everyone harmonious and happy.

At the end of a month of this practice, they left for Southern California and immediately contacted a real estate office near the ocean. They were told that there was only one listing with their specifications and were taken to see the house. Mrs. B. could not believe her eyes when the agent stopped beside a corner house with lots of tall trees. She was further astonished to find the outer walls were almost entirely glass and that the living room windows opened as huge sliding walls on both the ocean and pool sides of the large room. The dining table was in the center of this wide opening and the feeling was that of living in an open garden surrounded by tall, enclosing shrubbery and flowers. Facing the west was the great, blue Pacific just below and toward the east was the lovely pool amidst flowering plants and a high wall. Both were enormously pleased with the prospect of moving the family there at the approaching end of the school year.

On their first day at the new house, the boys were so excited they couldn't wait to get into the pool, but neither knew how to swim so Mrs. B. started teaching them at once. Within three weeks they both swam like fishes and were joined by the neighborhood children, all of whom had the time of their lives. They also swam in the ocean where the elder son became strong, healthy and robust.

This is an excellent example of predetermining the future by creating a mental blueprint and living in the subjective experience of its fulfillment until it objectifies into the outer world of the senses.

You are the architect and builder of your own life and destiny.

— A. A. Montapert

Revising the Facts

Knowingly or unknowingly, man initiates his own circumstances.

— The Author

Brian J. was told by his doctor that he had a terminal case of cancer and at best might have three-to-six months to live. Believing the good doctor, his condition promptly made a dramatic decline and he was expected to make his final exit any day when a friend whom he had not see for years came to visit.

Brian was pleased to see him and remarked that he looked considerably younger than when they had last met several years ago. His friend answered that it was all due to a change in his thoughts and attitude. He explained how he had seemingly reversed the aging process by the practice of healthy self-programming.

Brian announced that it was too late for him as his doctor had just confirmed his terminal condition. But his friend, recognizing that he knew nothing of the laws of the mind and the principles of cause and effect, began to explain the powers of belief. Brian was greatly impressed to learn that there are several clinics in the U.S. that practice a completely different form of health care that includes disciplines of the mind, diet, exercise, love and laughter. And that each was directed by a doctor who had revised his practice from traditional medicine to celebrating the glorious harmonies of life and involving his patients in this positive attitude.

Brian asked how one could get information about such doctors. By calling the American Medical Association (AMA) and asking about natural health care and clinics, his friend explained, adding, "I'll be glad to do it for you if you like," and he did. At the same time, he learned that chiropractors are often knowledgeable about such places and activities, and that some health food stores have literature on the subject.

In short, his friend helped him to find just such a wholistic clinic and in less than a week he was enrolled in the center's healing program.

When his own doctor examined him some time later, he was awestruck to find him thin but with no trace of disease and remarked happily that only a miracle could account for such a dramatic transformation.

Brian now helps others to recover and has a bright new lease on life. When asked his age he answers that age is a matter of the mind, and if you don't mind, it doesn't matter.

What you did yesterday creates today's circumstances.

— Thomas Blandi

Health

Your medicine is in you and you do not observe it. Your ailment is from yourself and you do not recognize it.

— **Sufi Hazrat Ali**

There is vast evidence that the quality of our thoughts, attitudes and our self-esteem is the quality of our health and experience. This has long been known to those who for untold centuries have understood the law of cause and effect, that condition equals cause.

To give regular attention to the undesirable in any form is to attune the subtleties of our lifeforces to destructive energies. We need only to observe our state of mental and bodily health to see the results of the causes that we have set in motion.

There is no medication that can heal a condition while its cause continues. And cause begins in the mind, either knowingly or unknowingly. It is impossible to be well and to be focused on sickness.

It is equally true that man experiences the quality of his dominant thoughts. If you would be harmonious and well, dear reader, it is essential that you fill your mind with all that is pleasant, constructive and desirable. There are noble causes and deeds, heroic acts and touching sacrifices for the good of others in abundance. The media overflows with all that is sordid and violent, but there are better choices for your time. It is naive to believe that you are not affected by that to which your mind is regularly exposed.

Do not allow others to tell you bad news, for this will generate destructive vibrations within you and lower your spirits. When family or friends attempt to tell you anything tragic or sinister, politely answer that you are practicing new mental habits and ask them to tell you instead, something happy and desirable. Be prepared with quiet and pleasant

89

answers, look for humor at every hand, and be your own master by remaining pleasant and cheerful, regardless of the situation.

If you are dead set on getting even, forgiveness is the only way that works. Holding a resentment does not even the score, it leaves you short-changed. No one can disturb us unless we allow it to enter into our emotions. We have a choice. Concentrate on remaining calm and harmonious at all times. If at all possible, try to be of service to others. It is highly effective to give in our mind that which we desire.

It is a disservice to yourself if you are in need and concentrate upon this, for it will sustain your condition. Thought reproduces its own likeness in our experience, so it is imperative that we fill our mind with healthy and happy thoughts. As R. W. Emerson wrote, "The measure of our mental health is the disposition to find good everywhere."

Yes, it is our thoughts and attitudes that cause us to feel tired, ill and weary—or light and spirited. If, in our state of exhaustion, someone were to bring us miraculous and thrilling good news, our mind would immediately transcend all awareness of fatigue and soar into carefree joy and wonder It is a proven fact that persons with a painful illness, too weak even to stand, were either relieved of their symptoms or tremendously improved after being exposed to lengthy and hilarious laughter.

Very seldom have I experienced any illness, but many years ago I had the flu. I had a high temperature and was barely able to breath; everything ached terribly. A friend and her New Zealand boyfriend came to visit. As a naval officer, he had collected amusing stories from all over the world and he told them energetically. At first, I was too ill to laugh; they held no humor for my aches and pains. He continued and I began to smile faintly. Little by little I was so distracted from myself that his humor caused me to burst out in explosive laughter. I assure you that before they left that evening, two hours of constant laughter had completely healed my illness. I felt light, free and happy.

Once, while lecturing four times a week in New York, I experienced laryngitis and had no voice at all. With only a few hours before lecture time, I began to feel panicky. There was no one to replace me and some of my followers had come from far out of the city. Finally realizing that I had no choice but to transcend my condition, I set about focusing on the ideal. Weakly at first, I began to imagine that I was on stage and speaking in a full and clear voice. In imagination, I repeatedly presented the subject that I had prepared and finally became completely unaware of my condition, so lost was I in its stories and examples. After continuing my silent lecture for over two hours, I tried my voice to see if there was one, and to my relief it sounded almost normal. While dressing and grooming myself I embodied a sense of radiant health and then I left for the lecture hall. Throughout the evening my attitude was that of super-abundant energy, feather lightness and soaring spirit. No one guessed that three or four hours earlier I could not make the faintest sound.

A healthy diet is also important, with whole grain breads and cereals, fresh, lightly cooked vegetables and fresh fruit. Study the chapter on the creative process, and in your mind, live in "the ideal."

I visualize you in perfect and radiant health, joyfully active in the field of your choice. Be peaceful, be happy and be loving, but most of all, in your creative imagination, experience the life of your dreams.

The good or ill of man lies within his own will.

— **Epictetus**

The White House

As within, so without, as above, so below.

— Hermes

Janet's aging parents owned no apartment or home of their own. Their modest rent was too high for their small monthly income and they lacked various simple comforts. Janet reflected over their hard lives and wished she could provide them with some measure of ease to offset so many sacrifices they had made for her benefit. Seeing no way to buy them a home on her small salary, she sadly wondered if there were not some way, some miracle that would enable her to help her parents.

One day Janet saw an announcement of classes taught by this author in New York's Steinway Concert Hall on the subject of fulfilling one's desires. She decided to attend one meeting to see if she found it interesting.

I taught the creative process of the mind and explained its function in detail. Janet was glad she came as she recognized for the first time that if she used her creative faculties properly, she could have whatever she wanted. Following the teaching, she set aside a fixed time of thirty minutes every morning in which she brought the vision of a lovely white house with rose vines growing around a nice porch where her parents could sit outside and enjoy the flowers and green lawn. She saw it on a large corner lot and noticed the white garage in the back garden.

Janet, who now attended every meeting, learned from my instruction that she should not visualize the house as in a distant city, but rather, bring the city around her presence. Forgetting where she actually sat in her "silent time," she imagined her surroundings to be the city of her parents, and that her own home was toward the south. In her mind, she was situated in the center of the action.

As Neville Goddard explained so marvelously in his book *Resurrection,* one should never project oneself elsewhere; rather, bring elsewhere here. And Janet did this in a spirited mood of joy and delight.

Bringing her parents faces before her, she heard them announce their great pleasure at her gift of the house. They loved the large corner lot and the spacious white porch with its climbing pink roses. She imagined again and again that she saw and heard the other family members stating their pleasure over their parents' new home.

No one knew or could ever have guessed that Janet had such a project in mind. And she, not relying upon the natural laws of our mind, put all her faith and trust in me. She could not understand how her attitude and practice could possibly provide the money to purchase the house, but she committed to this mental project her very best and faithful efforts.

Janet had no religion, but she remembered her father, no church member himself, quote from the Bible something about believing in whatever you desire, so she practiced believing that she had already bought the house.

She found that after every practice the house became more and more real. It seemed to take on substance and move from an idea in the mind to a house in the city. She was fascinated by her growing confidence in the matter and now believed that just such a house actually existed.

So every morning she strengthened her mental blueprint by actually experiencing all the sensations that would naturally accompany her dream come true. After two weeks, she recognized that her vision grew more objective and she could see the white house in her mind's eye. Details of the house began to take form and she could see and feel them becoming more and more a reality.

One day Janet's office manager announced that she was retiring and asked if she would like to be recommended as her replacement—at a salary twice that of her present earnings. Janet was spellbound with joy and excitement. The office manager knew that with some advance training Janet would be the ideal person for this responsibility and explained this to their employer. Janet was replaced in her own work and became the assistant to the office manager until the latter's retirement.

Now with her doubled salary, Janet knew she could buy the house for her parents. Yet there were other considerations; with her new responsibilities she could not take the time off to go house hunting in another city. Finally, she arranged for others to help her parents locate a suitable house and a few weeks later she drove to their city for the weekend to see and discuss the possibility of its purchase.

She had not specified to those who were to find it that she hoped it would be white or that it should have a front porch with climbing roses, a white garage in the back garden, or that it should be on a corner lot. But to her great astonishment when they went to look at the house, it had precisely those features. All agreed that it was well worth the price and the papers were prepared for her signature.

A few weeks later, she returned to the house, found her parents nicely settled, and celebrated the completion of her subjective mental blueprint having crystallized into objective fact.

Every idea carries its own solution. We can seldom see how something will work out, but if we begin by assuming that it is already complete and resolved, the means will present themselves.

Belief creates its verification in fact.

— William James

A Flaming Heart

Before water will generate steam it has to boil. Every great
achievement is the story of a flaming heart.

— A. B. Zutavern

Conception occurs in the rise of temperature, and so it is with all
desire and fulfillment. Thought is the architect of desire, but feeling gives
it life. Every time we think happily about our desire as already realized,
we add life to its formation and development. Feeling is creative energy,
and the more we join emotion to our inner vision of fulfillment, the
sooner our desire will be realized.

All we see around us—all that man has created— first began as ideas
that were embellished with vision and feeling. While a small desire that is
relatively easy to attain requires very little additional energy and heat, we
can readily see that a mammoth project would require the energy of a
flaming heart, and a longer period of conscious and subconscious
gestation.

We may wish and hope, pray and expect interminably for the
fulfillment of our desire, but unless we give it life by activating the
creative process, it will remain as an unfertilized egg.

Many studies have been made of the greatest achievers of history,
and it is clearly evident that they were all men and women with hearts
flaming for their cause and purpose.

We might feel that we have no such driving and compelling desire,
and are therefore incapable of achieving our goal. Happily, we have all
the resources by which the necessary forces can be activated. By
accepting our desire as already realized, then regularly experiencing in
imagination that which we would be doing and feeling were it actually
present, we can initiate the equivalent energy and spirit. It is important

that these principles and laws be repeated again and again, that you may associate them with all aspects of your life.

You would be wise to read and reread this book until you have mastered the creative process. Neville, the late author-teacher, related the story of a man who was despondent at being unable to support his family. Although he was unemployed and had no funds, when he heard of the wonders derived from Neville's teaching, he borrowed the modest fees for the class and his book *Resurrection* and read and reread it for weeks. In order to sustain his inspiration he carried it everywhere with him. He told Neville that he read it until he memorized every word. As a result of his daily practice of imagination he became the head of a real estate firm and the owner of various valuable properties. This is a classic example of combining daily imagination and its byproduct, a Flaming Heart.

Your achievement shall be in proportion to your desire.

— **Evelyn Underhill**

About Face

We are spinning our own fate, good or evil.

— William James

James found himself on the threshold of bankruptcy. Stressed to the limit and desperate, he thought only of failure and despair. Daily, he announced to his wife that their life savings had all been used in trying to save their long-declining business. He had mortgaged both their home and business property and soon, he knew they would both belong to the bank. What could he do? To whom could he turn? His dilemma compounded daily.

One day in utter despair, James looked up into the bright face of one of his suppliers entering his office. "I was just passing and thought I'd drop in to see why you haven't ordered anything for so long." "No business, no money," answered James. "See this stack of overdue bills? When the phone rings, it's not orders—if s creditors. How can I order anything?"

"James," said the supplier, "I just attended a lecture by a woman who teaches the creative process of the mind and she says that experience and circumstance are the mirror of our mind. You brought this disaster on yourself; I've seen it coming for a long time. Your attitude is down on everybody and everything. You created a miserable environment for your employees and you surely don't inspire your customers to come back. No wonder that you have no business. How do you expect to succeed when you're doing all the wrong things?"

James angrily replied, "But I've given my sweat and blood for this business. If s not my fault—it's the economy. Business is just bad all over." "Not so," said the salesman, "most of my clients are making money; I can tell by their regular orders." "Well, its too late now," lamented James. "I see no way to avoid bankruptcy, and with that both the house and business go."

"Not necessarily," answered the salesman. "If you'll listen, I'll tell you what the woman said. It sounds reasonable to me and I'm now using it myself." Sighing, James surrenders. "What have I got to lose?"

"See that pile of bills? I want you to imagine that they are all checks. You must change your whole attitude; and if you'll cooperate, I'll help you climb out of this impasse." James agrees to do anything. "Good," said the salesman, "now you must spend every free moment doing something creative. I want you to write letters of appreciation to every one of your clients. I want you to start looking for reasons to compliment each one of your employees, even for being on time. Chat with them a little every day, ask about their families. Ask if they have any ideas about better ways of doing things. Encourage them to come to you with suggestions. Try to make them feel appreciated; everybody needs it. Now they work strictly for their paycheck. Change your attitude and get them to work for the benefit of the company, which will secure their jobs." James went home that evening with hope in his heart.

The more he thought about it, the more he realized that the salesman was right: if we want to be successful we must think "success." He talked it over with his wife who agreed to practice with him and try-to save the business by changing their entire mental attitude.

Following the principles and laws of the creative process, James made a full three-hundred-and-sixty-degree turnaround and directed all his energies into doing in his imagination all that he would be doing were his desire already fulfilled. In his mind he went to the bank daily with a full money pouch, and saw the figures grow in his bank statements. He called clients for a friendly chat and offered incentives for their business. He made himself both visible and friendly among his few clients. He now showed a sincere interest in his employees, communicated with them daily and encouraged their suggestions, and they responded cheerfully.

James and his wife rose half-an-hour earlier every morning and rehearsed in the silence of their mind seeing, hearing, conversing and doing all that they considered ideal. They practiced sustaining their healthy and prosperous inner visions throughout the day. And in the evening before their early bedtime they invested another half-hour in self-programming a prosperous and growing business and a happy and enriching life.

After one month of "about face" practice, there were already small signs of change. Six months later, they were making regular payments on their bank loans. Today, James' firm is not only the leading company of its kind in his city, but it has branches all across the nation.

Now he knows that our dominant thought patterns and established mental habits are the blueprints of our experience.

Mind is the master power that molds and makes,
And man is mind and evermore he takes
The tool of thought and shaping
what he wills Brings forth a thousand joys,
a thousand ills,
He thinks in secret and it comes to pass,
Environment is but his looking-glass.

— James Allan

Fame and Fortune

Keep your head cool, your feet warm, your mind busy.
Talk and act like a winner and in time you will become one.

— Stephen Harte

Coming from a large and very poor family, a young man found his every path blocked due to lack of funds. Bright, ambitious and eager for a quality education with the highest degrees, he found that trying to work, study and do his own research was a great challenge.

It required almost everything he could earn in his part-time work to pay the high tuition, even though he denied himself the smallest comforts. It was a time of great sacrifice, menial work, and late-night studies. Little pleasures, such as a meal in a modest restaurant or going to a movie, were luxuries far beyond his means. Apart from this, of course, he needed clothing, books and other essentials.

So painful was this struggling period of his life that he resolved to rise above it. If others climbed to stature and position, so would he. He now turned his thoughts away from poverty and need and began to self-program abundance and a rewarding and respected position.

To clarify, concentrate and strengthen his resolve, he composed an affirmation with which he identified daily as follows: "I have a lavish, stable and dependable income, consistent with integrity and mutual benefit."

Faithful to his resolution, he began to live in his dreams as though they were already realized. This relieved him of the heavy emotional burden upon his spirits.

At last, he graduated from the highest academic studies in his field and confronted the fiercely competitive job market. Now armed with his creative mental habits, he was sure that he would climb the ladder to success.

Being exceptionally bright, talented and resourceful, he created his own opportunity and began his ascent toward fulfilling his dream.

The more he identified with his goal as already realized, the faster he progressed.

Every year he found himself on a higher rung of the ladder until he became the president of California Institute of Technology ("Cal Tech") in Pasadena, California.

He was none other than the world-famous scientist, Robert Millikan.

You cannot fail if you see yourself as successful.

— John Scott

Desire and Self Image

We are always acting out some role in life. Why not select the role of a successful person and rehearse it?

— William Marston

George C. was trained as an engineer and put himself through college washing dishes, mopping floors and taking out the garbage in the college cafeteria. At last, he graduated and set out to find a job with his new degree. He sensed that his interviewers were not impressed with him although he did not understand the reason. Strangely, he felt the same reaction from each interview. Something was surely wrong, but George couldn't imagine what it was. After each rejection his confidence weakened and this pattern continued month after month.

Still living at home because his part-time job doing dishes could not sustain him elsewhere, George grew increasingly discouraged. Any discerning eye could see in his body language and facial expressions total frustration and complete absence of self-esteem. Listless and without an appetite, George withdrew from the pain of the outside world that had rejected him and spent more and more time brooding in his room. His parents were alarmed but not understanding the problem, they could be of no help.

His mother put the want ad section of the daily paper in his room, but George had lost hope. He couldn't face any further rejections.

One day, George saw a television program about a story very similar to his own and the man had resolved his problem by going to a psychologist. But George had no money; how could he avail himself of this counsel? Continuing to think about it, he remembered that in the classroom next to one of his was a professor of psychology. Drawing upon what little courage he had left, George waited outside the professor's class and timidly spoke to him as he came out. Recognizing at once that

George had a problem, he said, "Come along, I'm on my way to the cafeteria; I'll listen over a sandwich."

George explained that he had graduated from the college almost a year ago, and had worked his way through school here in the kitchen with dishes and cleaning. The professor saw at once that George had identified himself with his work; although he had a degree in engineering, his self-image was that of a dishwasher. Washing dishes was a worthy occupation, explained the professor, but he was presenting himself in his engineering interviews with the demeanor and attitude of his cleaning job, giving cross signals to his prospective employers. His qualifications were good but he seemed more like their messenger than the person who had earned them.

The professor explained to George that he was lacking in self-esteem, that he didn't feel worthy to work alongside the other engineers. His feeling of inadequacy was obstructing his way. An adult education class was about to begin in a local high school and the professor suggested that George look into it; it was called *Self-Esteem.*

George left feeling hopeful and followed through on the night classes. Part of the training included silent identification with a useful and honorable role in life. Soon he began to see and feel differently about himself. He stood erect and walked tall. He practiced the feeling of having an ideal job and being respected among his colleagues. Continuing his part-time job in the kitchen and doing it as thoroughly as possible, he now identified himself as a highly valuable engineer with a job that he loved. He invested all his free time in rehearsing his new self-image and in the silence of his mind he gave full attention to being a great asset to his company.

George's parents remarked that he had become a new person and he noticed that people now treated him with respect. He found that he liked people and enjoyed the camaraderie of new friends. Feeling ready to become involved in his own field, he secured an interview and this time was very well prepared.

The week before the appointment, he had invested all his extra time in silently celebrating his new job. Now, he did not mention salary but only that his heart was set on working for this particular firm and that he would make every effort to see that his department was exemplary in the company. He had picked up literature and brochures about their activities and was knowledgeable about their products and services. He was spirited and confident and he sensed that his interviewer was impressed.

To be sure, George was engaged as an engineer and has made a noteworthy contribution to his department. Recognizing the creative powers of imaginal experience, George now used it in all aspects of his life. He developed a warm, friendly and effective working style with his colleagues, among whom there is mutual respect and camaraderie. A happy and fulfilled team leader in his company, he has a healthy and harmonious family and teaches them and others how to use the magical powers of their mind to achieve their goals and enrich their lives.

Fully ninety-five percent of our behavior, feeling and response is habitual. Healthy self-images do not bruise easily.

— **Maxwell Maltz, M.D.**

Ideas

An idea, in the highest sense of that word,
cannot be conveyed but by a symbol.

— Samuel Taylor Coleridge

All language is but symbols of ideas and concepts. And even ideas and concepts are but symbols of things, states, and conditions. Thus, all thought and all speech, as well as the written word, are synthetic in that they are psychological signs or characters, ideographs representing something else.

H.G. Wells maintained that human history is in essence a history of ideas.

Yes, our quality, character and caliber are equal to our most intimate companions: the ideas that we savor, enhance, act upon, or store away in that vast and mysterious repository that we call the subconscious. Even if never acted upon, noble, expansive and enriching ideas are better company than mingling with mediocrity.

"He is the greatest artist who has embodied in the sum of his works, the greatest number of the greatest ideas," wrote John Ruskin. Such ideas do not arise upon command, they should be courted as a lover; and according to the wisest of minds, no better way has been found than that of assuming the presence of one's fulfilled desire, then mentally living in its consequences. Our subconscious will present the appropriate idea in its proper time.

Every idea carries its own solution; if we find it appealing, let us be not only its host, but its joyful embodiment. This quickens and vivifies its likeness in our lifeforce field, adding its enriching tones to our unique and silent song of life.

It is a lesson which all history teaches wise men, to put trust in ideas, and not in circumstances.

— Ralph Waldo Emerson

Finances

Money is a terrible master, but an excellent servant.

— P. T. Barnum

Money, as all else, represents its equivalent in energy and we are either growing or diminishing in this commodity. Most of us feel unfulfilled in this domain, for which there are two major reasons:

1. We merely wish and hope for greater supply which strengthens and sustains its likeness: more wishing.

2. We pursue money as the means to fulfillment.

Both these approaches are in conflict with the natural order. To wish is to imprint in our subconscious a blueprint of lack and absence. As thought is creative in its own likeness, wishing and hoping perpetuate themselves.

Pursuit is an inner thrust and is met with equal resistance. To run after a desire is to find that it eludes us.

Unaware of the creative process, most of us obstruct our own path with the false assumption that before we can fulfill our desire we must first pursue and acquire the necessary means—money. This is to work against our own best interests. If we are to succeed in any endeavor we must proceed by the laws of its nature.

Effect equals cause so we must learn to initiate the proper cause for the desired effect. In our learning we must come to recognize that striving, pursuing, willing and forcing are out of harmony with the natural order of life; the resulting discord will equal the extent of our force.

Naomi G. learned of our superb endowment of creative faculties and, deciding to put it to the test, she chose as her goal the acquisition of

111

$100,000 net. She worked outside her home and decided to so organize her day as to give her half-an-hour each night and morning to experience in imagination the consequences of her desire as being already present.

By ignoring and transcending her state of lack, and in imaginal experience thinking, feeling and acting as she would if her desire were fulfilled in the present, she established a mental blueprint which the creative faculties prepared to reflect in her outer experience. And so vividly and joyfully did she embody her wish as fulfilled, that in just under three months she was invited by a television studio to host a program of cooking classes, for which, after taxes, she received precisely $100,000.

What you habitually think largely determines what you will ultimately become.

— **Grenville Kleiser**

Consciousness and Mind

Consciousness is the root, embodied experience the flower.

— The Author

Generally, little or no thought is given to the important distinction between consciousness and mind. We know that our mind, in its vast complexity, is the accumulated knowledge of our multifaceted brain. We know that it has a beginning and therefore must have an ending. There is clear evidence that it begins to form even before our birth.

The mind is formed in relation to its human genes and its environment, and functions within a range of intellectual frequencies particular to our so-called physical plane of being. It is individual and unique, and it is also multi-tiered.

Consciousness is a dramatically different matter. Having no beginning, it can therefore have no ending. It cannot accumulate, diminish, nor in anyway change or respond to any form of stimulus. It is all-pervasive, inseparable and impersonal; yet, it is the source, the foundation, the background for individuality and personality, as well as all else. It experiences neither birth nor death and is unaffected by either.

Consciousness has no faculties, therefore no means of assessment, reason or reaction to our experience. It has no involvement in our likes or dislikes, our pain or pleasure, our life or death. These things are not of its nature. It is as impersonal as the light of the sun or that of a lamp. It has no distinguishing capacity. Yet without it there could be neither man nor universe. Another term for its nature is "Infinite Awareness," and so elusive is its presence, it is not perceived by our mental faculties, from which they and all existence derive.

So accustomed is the mind in its outward focus to perceive and distinguish the surrounding phenomena, it does not recognize conscious awareness as a precondition. It would seem that awareness and perception are one and the same thing, or at least that they are fused into one and the same thing, but this is not the case. Even when our mind attempts to perceive the distinction between itself and consciousness, the latter is so subtle it seems nowhere to be found.

Here lies the difference between the intellectual approach of seeking knowledge from the objective plane and that of learning to go directly to its source in the subtleties of the subjective domain of silence. We of the Western World have not been taught that all knowledge is accessible from both directions. Though the scientist who works in his lab and the sage who sits alone in some remote area in deep silence may each come to the same understanding, the sage has the greater advantage, as he can reach knowledge far beyond the capacity of the intellect.

Conscious awareness could be likened to an infinite and invisible field of countless idea-seeds or seed-concepts which rise out of this subjective psychical state to flower in the objective outer world of so-called substance and experience. It is a fascinating and miraculous process, and not at all as it appears.

Thus, we see that consciousness is not a part of our mind, but its true source—its root, its origin, its foundation. Yet they function together as a unit, and though consciousness is the base, nothing can reach its elevation.

Sometime in the not distant future, educators will be aware that there is nothing more fundamental or useful than to study and teach the laws of silence. The greatest minds of whom there is record became great not by developing the intellect, but in learning to use it to transcend itself. The two should go hand in hand. Both are needed.

It is interesting to observe the vast differences between the mental development and conscious awareness of the three major groups of human evolution: the primitive bushman, restrained only by law from his cannibalistic practice; the great majority of humanity, attempting to broaden its understanding and to advance on all fronts; and, the all-too-few enlightened sages of the world, to whom the mysteries have revealed their secrets.

Even centuries are a short period in which to discern any noteworthy progress in the evolution of the mind. It seems to advance in groups and subgroups. Ours appears to be the age of science and technology, and it could be rightly said that our advances in these fields surpass our ability to live together in peace and mutual service. We are painfully lacking in the teaching and practice of ethical culture. Yet, great strides are being made in the compassionate endeavor of some segments of the human family.

Dr. Raynor Johnson, astrophysicist and retired Master of Queen's College, Melbourne, Australia, with whom I had the honor of addressing a large New York audience, asks: "Where is consciousness? Is not consciousness extra-spatial? It is a fundamental idea which cannot be defined, yet without it nothing else can be defined."

We wonder about its source and location, but it has no source and its presence is everywhere. It is the one and only question without an answer. It is unanswerable. All else is knowable.

So important, yet so subtle is the nature of consciousness, not even the most brilliant intellects can find a way to approach it. It has long been discussed by the most learned of men, but with no conclusive or satisfying results. Each side remains with its opposing views.

The problem lies in our mental frequencies; they are much too weak to penetrate into the lowest and highest dimensions of manifest existence. Yet we each have the capacity to transcend our intellect and experience the very essence of the mysteries. One certainty: no amount of discussion can resolve the matter. It is equal to the attempt to light the heavens with a match.

Manly Hall said of the process: "Man first passes from a subconscious unity to a semiconscious diversity, and then from the semiconscious diversity to a conscious unity." In other words, down through the lowlands of involution, across the planes of evolution, and up through the highlands back to our source.

Meanwhile, be kindly, be loving and be happy, for our thoughts are creating the quality of our experience. Awareness contains the universe.

The mystery of man is imperceptible to the senses or to any human power.

— St. John of the Cross

"I Meditate my Class"

Meditation is a clarifier of a beclouded mind.

— Unknown Tibetan Sage

During my twice-weekly lectures on the nature of reality and the creative process of the mind, in which I included disciplines of meditation, I asked from time-to-time for examples of the effective use of my teaching. One night, a delightful young man who had become a "regular," stood and related the following story.

As a member of the New York teaching force, he was assigned to one of the city's most notoriously delinquent schools. His class of ten-to-twelve-year-olds was beset with bedlam; so belligerent, disrespectful and impossible was the group that no teacher would remain in their classroom.

The young man had been briefed by the principal who had given up hope of ever controlling their fighting, swearing and destruction of school property.

Clearly the young man had inherited a classroom disaster. Inspired by my promise of truly miraculous results if one would learn and practice the law of assumption, he established an early morning discipline of what he called "meditating my class."

Knowing all too well the disorderly behavior of these youngsters, our young man followed the teaching of seeing them in the silence of his mind, not as they were, but in the ideal. Sitting comfortably in his living room, he brought the class before his mind's eye. He imagined everyone nicely groomed, quietly enjoying their lesson and behaving in the most exemplary manner. He walked among them warmly and respectfully and cheerfully praised their smallest effort. Recognizing that their unfortunate lives (often without a father) contributed to their lack of respect and suppressed desire for affection, he decided to become a silent caring father to the class. Following his meditation, he would leave for school.

Within one week, he noticed small changes in their behavior and attitude. Encouraged by this initial improvement, he persisted in his approach. Gradually, the children responded to his respect, his sincere and personal interest in each of them, and his praise and affection.

Instead of remaining in front of his class in an attitude of authority and presenting the lesson in a cold and academic manner, our young man walked among the aisles touching the children on the arm or shoulder in a warm and friendly fashion. His cheerful regard and sincere interest in each member of the class was new to their experience. He looked for even the smallest reason to praise them. Knowing that he must find a way to gain their interest, he sat on the front edge of his desk and told them stories worked around the lesson. The class loved his storytelling and began to enjoy some aspects of school for the first time. Day by day, as he earned their respect and confidence, they began to work, not for themselves, but to please their teacher.

Week by week, he continued "meditating his class" before leaving for school, experiencing it in the ideal. In his mind he saw them enjoying learning together and everyone was happy. Holding to this image, he saw a steady improvement in their attitudes and their efforts.

Within a few months there was to be a school-sponsored bus trip to the nation's capitol, so their teacher told them fascinating stories about the city and important people and events in its history. Before the date of their leaving they had acquired considerable knowledge and were eager and well prepared for an exciting learning experience.

As the result of repeatedly imagining in detail happy and spirited, but well-behaved children, the trip was precisely that, and everyone had a great time. In fact, the teacher's report to the principal brought a special acclaim for their class and honors at the end of the school year.

I submit to educators from preschool to the highest level of study, that by following the example of the bright young man of this story, they can create in their own environments an atmosphere of pleasure in learning that will enhance the lives of both instructor and student. And this can be enriched to a lifelong appreciation of the teacher, as well as the effective results of the knowledge acquired.

I remember with dearest affection my fifth-grade history teacher. It is doubtful that in those early years she had any precise knowledge of the creative process of the mind, but she used it superbly, for it is an innate endowment.

Perhaps the most important of her outstanding qualities was that of showing by her smiling expression, the tone of her voice and her general manner, that "she liked us." This is magical to students and elicits their desire to please their instructor—whether it is a class of children or adults. It acts as sunshine and fresh air to the spirit. Her attitude attracted the full attention of the entire class, and except when she asked for a response, we were still and silent, our minds alert and eager to absorb her every word.

So fully concentrated was each student upon her instruction that we remembered everything she told us, and the grades for the frequent tests she was required to give were always high; in fact, most of us earned top grades. Another interesting factor was our total lack of stress about the exams. Due to the teacher's skill in presenting the lessons, we were so interested and familiar with the material that we all competed with each other to earn the highest score.

Through all my years in the classroom she stands out as a shining example of the mutual pleasure that can and should pervade every learning environment. If only she were still alive and I could hug her and honor her with the praise that she deserved. But we were too young and didn't understand the concept or manner of expressing our affection. Perhaps the best and most rewarding appreciation for her efforts was that of our spontaneous response when the bell announced the end of the class period: Everyday, with disappointment and regret, we all sighed, Oh, no... so eager were we to remain in her presence.

Success comes to those who are success conscious.

— Napoleon Hill

Castles in the Sky

Hold a picture long and steady in your mind's eye and
you will be drawn to it.

— Dr. Harry Fosdick

Leroy W. was born and raised in New York's Harlem where he
worked as an engineer in its subway system. Five days a week he took the
subway to and from his work, which was three floors below the streets of
the city. He hated spending his days underground and wished he could
work in the very top of one of the city's great skyscrapers. A part of his
train route was above ground and he chose one of the tallest towers as his
ideal place of employment because it reminded him of a castle in the sky.

Leroy had been thinking about his castle for some time but only in a
kind of now-and-then fashion, for he didn't know how to go about getting
a job that he feared might be beyond his qualifications. But one day
something happened on the subway that put his mind in high gear. The
person sitting next to him was reading a book that lay open on her lap,
and Leroy noticed that the chapter was entitled "Dream Your Way To The
Top." This so excited his imagination that he felt the message was meant
just for him.

Now he began to use every minute of his subway ride to concentrate
on his dream. Besides the one hour, going and coming, his thoughts were
occupied with his castle during his every free moment.

One day as he was on his way to work he noticed the newspaper of
his seat companion was opened to the section of classified ads and in
clear view he read "Help Wanted, Engineer." Recognizing the address of
his castle, Leroy's heart almost jumped into his throat. As he tried to see
the telephone number to call, the man hastily folded the paper, rushed
toward the exit and disappeared—but Leroy had seen the address.

Nervous and fearful that someone else might get "his job" before his lunch break, he dashed over to the building and asked an attendant where to find the office of the engineer. In a moment, Leroy was facing his hopeful new boss. He explained that he was on his way to work and asked if the job could be held open until he returned during his lunch break. The engineer said he expected to interview at least several more applicants before making a decision.

Leroy went on to his job, his heart beating faster in fear that someone else might have higher qualifications and that he might not be the lucky man. His fears mounted throughout the morning; what if this, and what if that, raced through his mind.

At last it was lunch time and Leroy dashed back to his castle in the sky and so great was his eagerness, and so clearly was his heart set on "his job," that the engineer sensed that anything he might be lacking in experience he would surely acquire in a hurry. Leroy pleaded his case but the engineer held his ground saying that he expected several other hopefuls and would let him know.

Returning to the underground tunnels of his work, Leroy was both excited and scared. Somehow it came to him that his best hope was to pretend that the job was already his and if he could believe it strongly enough, surely his dream would come true. He decided at once to rise above his fears and pretend that he was happy. Yes, he would inwardly celebrate that it was he whom the engineer had selected, and he tried to sustain the feeling of his desire as already realized.

It was Leroy's first effort at creative daydreaming, and he wasn't quite sure that he was going about it right. All he knew was the chapter title "Dream Your Way To The Top"; there hadn't been time for him to read the HOW. He knew no other way than to follow his instincts. Every child knows how to daydream, he thought, so it must be instinctive. But assuming that adults were supposed to outgrow their childhood practices, he hadn't daydreamed in years. Yet there must be something to it, he decided, for it was written in a book. He would give it his best try, for this was his chance of a lifetimes—to go from underground to the top of the city. "Yes," he vowed, "I'm going to DREAM MY WAY TO THE TOP."

Several days passed. It was not an easy task to stay above his fear and to be faithful to his assumption that the job was his. In his mind he worked in the new place. He imagined himself wearing the uniform of the engineering staff, he mentally rode the elevators basement to roof, he looked out over the great metropolis and saw the international airport in the distance. He spent all his free time doing in imagination all that he would be doing were his dream already realized. He carried on silent conversations, heard his boss compliment him on his good work. Twice a day on the subway he spent the hour imagining he was going and coming from his new job.

A few days later, he received a call from the head engineer asking him to return for a final interview Leroy's dream came true; not only was he employed in his castle in the sky, but he later succeeded to chief engineer when his boss retired.

To shorten the interval between desire and realization we should make our "silent time" a real love affair with our project, that we may look forward to our next practice. Soon the effects of this "happy time" will carry over into longer periods of our day, until all we think and feel is established in the new conditions.

Yes, castles in the sky are accessible to each of us if we will build them on the firm foundation of living daily in their happy consequences.

If man would endeavor to live the life of his imagination and his dreams he would meet with a success unexpected in common hours.

— Henry Thoreau

Destiny

Every man's fate is in his own hands.

— Sidney Smith

Do you believe in destiny? Do you feel dear friend, that the pattern of our life is preordained? Is it already designed and laid out?

According to many of the greatest minds of whom there is any record, we predetermine our own destiny by the quality of our every thought, word and action. William James, Professor of Philosophy at Harvard, noted that "We are spinning our own fate, good or evil."

Yes, unless there is a dramatic change in our mental habits, our destiny can be quite accurately self-predicted. True, we inherit aptitudes and predispositions from our genes and environment that influence our destiny, but inexorably, the determining factor in the quality of our future is the quality of our thoughts.

If our attention is focused predominantly upon that which is life-enhancing, both our present and our future will reflect the harmony of the natural order of life. This, of course, is true of its opposite as well.

In order to understand fate and destiny, it is essential to have some insight into the universal laws of cause and effect, which govern all existence. Cause is not self-initiating; it requires an activator to set it into motion. Things and conditions do not create themselves. To believe in fate or predetermined destiny implies that someone or something has charted the course of our lives, which would be a very naive assumption.

We are always the potential master of our destiny, yet we may not be exercising this freedom. In this way, we have little or no free will. We are only as free as the quality of the natural laws of the mind that we invoke by our thoughts, attitudes and actions. Except for the encoded traits of our inherited genes and environmental influence, our life at birth, is as an unwritten book. It is our choices that fill in the pages.

Man has no other destiny than the one he forges for himself.

— Jean-Paul Sartre

Good and Bad Luck

Shallow men believe in luck.

— Ralph Waldo Emerson

Recent advances in technology have revealed that the principles and laws of the mind are as precise and dependable as those of mathematics. It is interesting that this has been known to the sages of the world since ancient times—not from intellectual brilliance, but from persevering disciplines of silence and concentration.

Abstract truths are more elusive to the academic approach. The contemplatives long ago found answers that are as yet unknown to science. Even primitive tribesmen knew of the precise movement of various celestial bodies invisible to sight. Their shaman or spiritual leader observed their cyclical changes in profound silence beyond the sense of sight. A recent television documentary showed this still to be true in today's world.

To the degree that our mental habits are in keeping with the natural laws of life, our experience will be harmonious, and of course the opposite is also true.

The causes of much of our experience, however, are deeply buried in our subconscious mind, well below recall, but it is clear that consciously or unconsciously, we initiate the causes and quality of our lives.

There is no mystery about the person who has a record of successes and whose life is richly fulfilled. He is evoking the appropriate laws for the desired effect.

The state of our subconscious conditioning is particularly evident in our relationships and in the workplace. Statistics now show who is accident-prone and who has the highest rate of absenteeism. Some large organizations now screen applicants for these favorable or unfavorable subconscious traits.

To the discerning eye, people are seen as states of consciousness, acting out their subliminal conditioning. If the quality of our lives is consistently pleasing, we should continue with our established thought patterns; if not, we would be wise to review and practice the teachings in the chapters on imagination. In so doing we will predetermine our own happy experiences and a fulfilling destiny.

Luck is fickle; fortune is self-made.

— The Author

Good and Evil

The good life is one inspired by love and guided by knowledge.

— Bertrand Russell

What do you think of good and evil, my friend? Actually, no such things really exist. As explained in the chapter "The Pairs of Opposites," they are differing degrees of harmony and discord. It is strictly a matter of evoking—either wittingly or unwittingly—those laws which result in that which is life enhancing or their opposite, those which are in conflict with the natural order of life. If they benefit all whom they affect, we call the action good; if they enrich some and harm others, we call the result evil. And of course there are myriad degrees between the two extremes.

When we understand the natural laws of the universe we see clearly, as stated elsewhere, that the nature and quality of the cause is the nature and quality of the effect. They cannot be separated one from the other except by the laws of revision or transmutation.

If we are experiencing something undesirable, we must understand that knowingly or unknowingly we have evoked by our action imperceptible laws that are in conflict with the natural order. We have all made this error repeatedly. Or we may have allowed someone else's unwise judgment to influence our own.

People want very much the same things. Some know how to fulfill their desires playing by the rules, while others ill-equipped with this knowledge, use the only means of which they are aware.

In short, good means "in harmony with the laws of life." Sin and evil mean "in conflict with the laws of life."

Evil is the lack of cooperation with the law.

— Donovan

Big Ben

Both king and servant are subjects of the clock.

— The Author

A San Franciscan couple, the man of whom had spent his life in his impassioned love of clocks and watches, had long dreamed of a trip to Europe to see the famous Big Ben in its towering landmark of London. They could have gone any time but Mr. G., who had become something of an historian, waited for an opportunity to be received and hosted by an Englishman who shared his knowledge and love of this field. But long years had passed and no such opportunity presented itself.

It was the habit of Mr. and Mrs. G. to read to each other after dinner and then discuss the subject. Mrs. G. announced that she had found a new book in the library by a London author on the subject of famous clocks and watches of the world, and that she had brought it home. This was their first contact with a contemporary author who lived in the city of the great clock tower.

That night after their reading, it occurred to Mrs. G. that they had never done anything but wish and hope for their dream to come true. She remarked that they should probably be doing something creative to make it happen. So it was decided that every evening after dinner they would read from the London author's book about clocks and then engage in a discipline of "creative silent time."

Settled in comfortable armchairs, they each began to imagine that they were in the city of London. They visualized the great clock tower of Big Ben from the many photographs they had seen and felt the thrill of realizing their dream. Bringing all their senses into play, they felt the street under their feet, surveyed the London skyline and watched the boats on the Thames.

They listened to the British accents of the passersby; they climbed the tiny winding stairs of the red double-decker buses and savored the view of the bustling dty from that great vantage point. And best of all, they each assumed that they were being escorted to the clock tower by a prestigious authority on the subject. Losing themselves in their creative imaginal experience, they embodied all the happy feelings that would naturally be present on this delightful trip abroad.

They set a minimum time of half an hour for their nightly practice, but found it so enjoyable they always lingered overtime. What a difference it made in their spirit, their attitude and their general outlook. They found themselves happier than they had been for years. And each time they practiced they felt more familiar with all aspects of the trip. Knowing that they would fly, they experienced being aboard the plane and visualized the attendants going about their duties. They watched an imaginary film about London; they walked in the beautiful city parks, visited the museums and attended a concert. And they took guided tours both within and outside the city.

After they had been practicing their creative imaginal experiences for about a month they received an invitation to a dinner party at the home of one of Mr. G.'s colleagues, who was himself one of the greatest authorities on famous clocks of the world. They were both delighted and talked happily of buying a copy of the London author's book to take to their host.

Sharing a knowledgeable interest in her husband's lifelong passion for time pieces, Mrs. G. also looked forward to the pleasure of joining the conversation on this highly specialized subject. At last, the evening arrived and Mr. and Mrs. G. were graciously received by their hosts, to whom they presented the book by the English clock connoisseur. And there occurred one of the most astonishing and brightest moments of Mr. G's life. The surprise guest of honor was the London author himself.

The Magic of the Mind

During the evening's conversation the two men established a spirited rapport and the Londoner urged Mr. and Mrs. G. to come to England, promising them a personal guided tour of the world famous landmark.

A few months later Mr. and Mrs. G. did precisely in the objective outer dimension of the senses, that which they had been rehearsing in their subjective imagination. Not only did their new friends honor them with a guided tour of the great clock tower, but they gave a lovely dinner party for them so they could meet several friends with their mutual interest.

Mr. and Mrs. G. walked in the lovely London parks, took the double-decker bus around the city, visited the museums, went to the theater, attended a concert and enjoyed several guided tours. All that they had rehearsed in the creative domain of imaginal experience became a reality.

On returning home, Mrs. G. went to the library, browsed among the books on creativity, and to her delighted surprise found a variety of interesting titles on the subject. She and Mr. G. added an expanding dimension of the mind to their nightly reading Now that they knew how to use their imagination to create the fulfillment of their desires, they began a delightful sequence of "desire and realization" that has enormously enriched their lives.

Rhythm and cycle turn the wheels of all existence.

— **The Author**

Prayer

One of mature spiritual insight knows that prayer is
not asking but rejoicing.

— The Author

There is much said about prayer and its value, but little about its true nature and process. There can be no true understanding of prayer without considerable knowledge and insight of the natural laws of the mind.

We know that many prayers go unanswered while the wishes and deep yearnings of many nonreligious people seem more frequently fulfilled.

He who prays addresses his request to some assumed higher authority who is believed to perceive, assess and either grant or deny his plea. If it is granted, he feels that it is a grace; if withheld, he believes himself to be unworthy.

Some five hundred years before biblical times the Greek poet Pindar wrote wisely, "I have many swift arrows in my quiver which speak to the wise, but for the crowd they need interpreters."

And so it is with prayer. All desire, whether prayer or otherwise, is either fulfilled or unrealized according to our correct or incorrect use of the creative process of our mind.

Fulfillment is a matter of belief, and belief is not instantaneous; it requires attention, practice and repetition. Belief in the truest sense means faithful assumption that that which is yet unperceived actually already exists.

In some Bibles, the translators have rendered the text: "Whatsoever things you desire, believe that you receive and you shall receive." In others, it is translated as: "Whatsoever things you desire, believe that *you have received and you shall have them.*"

The latter is correct as far as it goes. But there is no clear instruction on how to proceed. It is incongruous to believe but continue to ask.

The process of belief is as follows: our desire should be embellished by thought into a detailed mental blueprint. It is the function of our subconscious mind to record our total experience, thus our blueprint is on file and the creative process has been activated. In order to strengthen and sustain belief in that which is not yet realized, daily practice is required. If we are practicing belief correctly we must look not with the eyes, but through the eyes and see things not as they are but as we desire them to be. In other words we must practice thinking, feeling and acting as though our desire were already fulfilled, and do in our mind and heart precisely that which we would be doing were it already manifest. This is applied belief: keeping the faith. This daily practice should be a joyous celebration.

This is true and effective prayer.

Prayer is the art of sustained imaginal experience.

— **The Author**

The Source of Knowledge

There is one mind common to all individual men.

— Ralph Waldo Emerson

As our faculties of cognition are focused outward, we wrongly assume that knowledge must be pursued in the outer, objective world. But the greatest minds of record have long known from their disciplines of concentration, that all knowledge is structured in myriad frequencies of all-pervading consciousness. Knowledge is everywhere, all about us, in the air, as it were.

I know from my own long hours of disciplined concentration in which I experienced varying levels of "direct knowing"—some sought, some spontaneous— that the quality of inner perception is infinitely superior to traditional academic learning.

Not only is it possible to find the answer or solution to a given question by acutely focused, one-pointed attention, but one can actually become and experience the state itself. As consciousness is singular and inseparable, and as it is all-encompassing— whether it is earth, air, sea or mountains, sun, moon or stars—each can be experienced either separate from, fused with, or beyond personality.

This can be achieved, but not in a manner of pursuit. By cheerfully and respectfully identifying with the phenomenon in a peaceful and enduring practice, this can and does occur. But we must be willing to pay its price of invested time.

As in all endeavors, one needs to prepare accordingly. The first step is to learn to still our wandering thoughts in order to remain one-pointed in our concentration. And this is not as simple and easy as it might seem. Few there are who can avoid intruding thoughts for even sixty seconds. Thoughts stir and ruffle the clarity of the mind as waves or ripples obscure the depth of a lake.

An excellent mode of practice for becoming master of your thoughts, if it attracts your interest, is that of setting a regular quiet-time of a certain length. Select a chair or sitting posture where you can be comfortable for at least thirty minutes (an hour or more is better), choose a time and place where you will not be disturbed, and begin with a cheerful attitude. Count your breath up to five and then return to one, continuing this repetition.

Do not try to avoid intruding thoughts. This is crucial. The more you resist them, the more your attention attracts them. Rather, court a sense of joy and self-praise when you succeed for however short a period. As thought and attention perpetuate and sustain their own likeness, your attention must be on the pleasure of success, now.

After you have learned to keep the mind still by counting, then lay this crutch aside and remain easily still and silent, free from thoughts for ever longer periods.

Soon you will be ready to begin your inner journey. At that time, and in a propitious mood of joyful, even loving reverence for the object of your attention, embody the state or condition. Sustain and endure in this identification, in "the feeling of lightness and pleasure."

If thoughts of your practice arise at other times, you should reinforce your attention with feelings such as "Isn't it wonderful?" It is highly important to be faithful to your "assumption" that ultimate fulfillment is present, here and now. And during some part of your practice you should rehearse experiencing that which you would be doing were it already realized. This imprints the subconscious mind, which, having no faculties of reason, produces your desired result.

Observe your sense of well-being carefully and adjust your practice time if indicated. Grooming your emotions to a constant sense of harmony and pleasure should accompany your practice.

We know that answers and solutions are sometimes revealed in a dream, or while we are relaxed and thinking of something quite different. The famous Austrian composer Franz Schubert said that his compositions

138

were "remembering melodies that were unknown to him or anyone else." To learn of the inner pathway to knowledge is a worthy end in itself and would certainly justify a disciplined practice for that purpose.

If you would know the answer to a particular question, it can be attained by assuming that it has already been revealed, then in thought and imagination act out that which would be the natural consequence. Be sure to add feeling to your daily practice. This would be an especially rewarding investment for those in research and business.

As science is among the most dedicated, persevering and noble of the arts, I thrill at the joys it will evoke when it is learned that there really is a pot of gold at the end of the rainbow—accessible in those peak experiences of "direct knowing."

We have found that there is a capacity for acquiring knowledge that transcends the sensory faculties.

— J.B. Rhine, Parapsychology Researcher, Duke University

Camaraderie

To know is nothing at all; to imagine is everything.

— Anatole France

Billy B's father loved to play golf and by the time his son was five or six years old, he began talking to him about the fundamentals of the game. For his tenth birthday his father bought him a child's club and putter, and they practiced in the back yard where together they kept a putting green as smooth as sheared velvet. Billy likes to remember how his father stood over him showing him how to hold the club, how to keep his left arm straight, to follow through and to keep his head down. He liked it from the beginning. He loved the stories his father told him about the famous players and the many fascinating things that occurred in the tournaments.

Soon, his father started taking him to the driving range on Saturday morning to hit balls and to putt. After an hour Billy left to join his friends while dad and his friends got down to serious business out on the greens.

Throughout high school, none of Billy's friends golfed, but well before graduation he was better at the game than most of his father's golf buddies who invited him to join them for eighteen holes on Saturday mornings. Billy was fast catching up with his dad.

The first year of college there was a lot of work and Billy had less time for golf, but in his sophomore year he went back to his weekly game with his father and friends.

A couple of Billy's classmates thought they would like to try their swing at the ball, so Billy started coaching them in his back yard where he had begun. Soon, they were meeting at the golf range to hit balls and were bitten by the bug. Enthusiasm spread and another student joined their trio, then another two. Now they were six and each was eager about their weekend game. Great camaraderie on the course: cars, girls, dating, money and studies—in that order. Life was a bright adventure and they each felt like winners.

All six graduated the same year and hoped to join the workforce in the same area. But two of the fellows could not find jobs and worried about their futures. Each of the two considered going to another part of the country where they had relatives. Everyone was saddened by their imminent separation.

Billy had an idea; he had been reading about the creative powers of imagination and suggested that they all meet twice a week at his place and join forces in seeing their two friends happily and ideally employed. One had no faith in such an abstraction and left the city. The other felt it wouldn't hurt to give it a try.

The five met and no one knew quite how to go about implementing the process. Wishing and hoping hadn't worked, so that couldn't be the way. Sending out resumes and making phone calls had been no more successful. At least they were eliminating the wrong approaches. Finally, one of them remembered reading somewhere that the best way of fulfilling a desire is to approach it by the same principles as that of acting. Acting is pretending, which activates the creative process. Another remarked that good actors must rehearse daily in order to feel themselves in their roles, and they recognized pretending as the way to belief. And wasn't it belief that caused things to happen? Yes, they would practice pretending they each had great jobs. Billy set the alarm clock for twenty minutes and all was silent.

At the end of their creative practice one remarked that he felt quieter and more peaceful than he could remember. They all said that their mind kept wandering, but when it came to their attention they brought it back to their purpose. The fellow who needed a job said he somehow felt more confident and lighter about the whole matter. Altogether, they were all pleased with their first retreat into the silence of creative imagination.

142

Two weeks later, after four sessions, it seemed that a great job almost fell in Billy's friend's lap. He hadn't even known about it. While standing in an open telephone booth, he overheard someone in the next booth say that he must put an ad in the paper to fill so and so's replacement. Our young man's heart beat a little faster. When the man hung up the phone, our recent graduate asked the type of work to which he had just referred. He was awestruck to hear that it was the very field in which he had just graduated. He took the man's card and called for an appointment. One week later he got the job and began at a salary above that which he had expected.

Now, sixteen years later, all are still fast friends. All have advanced in their careers and when anything on the horizon approaches an impasse, they get their heads together to concentrate on the ideal solution having been already resolved. This led to their using their natural creative endowment in all aspects of their lives; they discussed and practiced it with their wives and taught it to their children. And as you would expect, they astonished other golfers with their consistently great scores.

They still play eighteen holes on weekends, and their families and careers are healthy and well established. All this they credit to their creative "silent time."

The human race is governed by its imagination.

— **Napoleon Bonaparte**

Man: A Structured Hierarchy

Man, how wonderfully and fearfully he is made.

— William Shakespeare

All manifest existence, from the smallest particle to the greatest systems of galaxies, is structured in an hierarchical order. Whether it be constellations, suns, moons and stars, or faculties, organs and nervous systems, placement on the ascending and descending scale are in the order of their significance and expendability.

Without the sun, there would be no solar system. Thus, it is the reigning power among its subordinates.

Without the organ of the brain, there could be no human experience. This elevates it to the ranking power of the human organism.

Second-in-command is the heart, which could not function without the unconscious nerve-centers of the brain, though some of the illumined sages reverse the order of the brain and the heart.

The body cannot function without a liver, so this is one of the high-ranking ministries. The kidneys, a bit more expendable, are next on the descending scale. The body can function without the lower organs of the spleen and the appendix as well as the reproductive system. Bone structure, muscle tissue, and skin are components or members of higher orders.

Each organ has its various ministries and functions that perform on an hierarchical scale, orbiting as it were, around their central power.

The highest faculty of that rarified and complex organ, the brain, is that of cognition and differentiation, without which, as stated above, learning or human experience would not be possible.

Among the five senses, for example, sight is the ranking power. The faculty of hearing would be the next descending office. As the sense of touch with its ability to feel is present and essential throughout the organism, it would outrank the faculties of smell and taste.

The head is the apex of importance to the entire body. The torso, more essential than its limbs; the arm, higher on the scale than the hand, the hand above that of a finger.

Throughout the universe, from the infinitesimal to the infinite, all phenomena are structured on a stratified and hierarchical order. This is evident in nature and families, in villages, towns, cities, counties, and states; in countries and in the governing bodies of each from the most powerful to the least prestigious.

In the countless phenomena of the universe there is an observable basic order, and only a few shapes and forms that are infinitely combined and repeated. The circle and sphere, the square and cube, the cylinder, and the triangle form the basis for many natural structures.

The human body, except for the sphere of the head, is composed of cylinders: the neck, the torso, the arms, fingers, legs, feet and toes are all of the same basic design.

It is fascinating to note that all forms and functions are structured in mathematical equations.

The height of an adult is about seven heads. His armspan, (from finger tip to finger tip), is about the measure of his height. From the elbow to the wrist is about the length of the foot, and so is the circumference of the fist.

The face is divided in thirds, with the crown and forehead occupying the first third, from the eyebrows to the nose the second third, and from the nose to the chin, the last third.

The space between the eyes is that of another eye. A line drawn straight down from the inner corner of the eyes will establish the width of the nose. A line drawn straight down from the outer corner of the eyes will touch the corners of the mouth. And the ears are positioned between the height of the eyebrows and the end of the nose. All other body-measurements correspond.

The development of man in his present state is the result of millions of years of change and adaptation. According to medical science, a human embryo of four- to five-weeks has the form of a fish, with a broad tail and traces of gills—a carry-over from the long sojourn up through the transformations of marine life. Shortly, it loses these and other aspects of its ancient formation and develops into its more evolved human form.

There are many characteristics of our early development that link us with other primates. Evidence of our climb up the ladder from our cave dwelling days, and our tribal life in the wild, include multiple births, our facial and body hair, and our dental molars, used for tearing meat before the age of utensils.

Our brain, organs, glands and bone structure are to science clearly in transition. According to some doctors, the adenoids, tonsils, appendix and spleen are parts nature is in the process of phasing out. Even the vast hierarchical tree of the cosmos is itself subject to the laws of change.

Nothing is still. All is in rhythmic cycle and motion. Poets sometimes refer to it as the cosmic dance, or the dance of life.

Man is a multi-dimensional being, structured in a sequence of diminishing density and opacity from without, inward. Since ancient times, mystics and contemplatives have called these planes astral, aether-ic, subtle or casual bodies, although there is some variance of their organization and function both in ancient and modern literature.

All phenomena emerge from concepts, principles, laws and processes, and pass down the scale of involution as they take on energy, form and progressively more substance. Science is still in its infancy in

147

the study of these elusive aspects of our nature— inaccessible to the microscope and scalpel—yet knowledge of them in various parts of the world predates the advent of writing.

Yes, hierarchy prevails from the lowest to the highest forms of life, from the microscopic to the infinitely vast.

Man himself is the crowning wonder of creation;
the study of his nature the noblest study the world affords.

— William Giles

Miracles

To me, every hour of the light and dark is a miracle;
every cubic inch of space is a miracle.

— William Shakespeare

In truth there are no such phenomena. Miracles, mysteries or the supernatural, are but results of laws with which we are not yet familiar. Once something is repeatable or thoroughly understood, it is no longer miraculous or mystical.

In every generation for thousands of years, there have been a few sages who understood and mastered the laws of so-called miracles, as is surely true today. But having undergone long years of disciplined training, a true master will not be found walking down the avenue in a business suit, nor engaged in any popular endeavor. If he is well-grounded and attuned to the natural order of life, the worldly pursuits of fame, fortune and possessions would hold no attraction. And if an authentic master could be found in some remote retreat or isolated hideaway, he would not exhibit his powers, nor even allow them to be known.

With regard to money or reward, the ideas are meaningless. They are not among his values. He is fulfilled and peaceful with few possessions and no special comforts, sitting alone in some unfrequented little corner of the world. Though he is master of laws yet unknown to science, he has no desire to use his powers and could not be persuaded. His answer would be silence.

That which the inexperienced and uninformed would not recognize is his indescribable inner wealth of "being consciously one with all existence." Being not merely aware of the highest virtues and treasures of existence, he is able at will to embody their differentiated experience. Not merely aware of infinite energy, light and sound, he is able to transcend all traces of human experience and actually become infinite energy, light

149

or sound, either separately or collectively. He is not only loving but love itself, not only blissful but bliss itself.

For him, time and distance are illusion, dark clouds in the mind. Past and future are nonexistent. The only time, is the eternal now. If he chose, he could attune his conscious awareness to any place or dimension and view, and experience or become, the subject of his interest. Still he would have no desire to display his powers. In fact, he would be very sure that no one knew except his spiritual teacher, if he had one.

One might ask, "Of what value or benefit can such a secluded life be to the needs of society?" This is a natural question, but the questioner asks from his limited and unenlightened knowledge; the master acts from his infinite wisdom and insight.

Another valid question might be: "Why does the master not use his powers to perform miracles of healing and relieve suffering?" Though it is difficult for our limited intellectual knowledge to comprehend, the role of a sage is to enlighten, to teach the laws of cause and effect, which enable us to make wise choices. It is the purpose of the specialists of the world to help resolve undesirable effects. The hard-earned wisdom of initiating only that which is desirable and harmonizing is of a far higher order. To paraphrase a biblical quotation, "The darkness cannot comprehend the light."

It might be rightly said that Jesus performed miracles and healed the sick. However, he did this only on occasion as an instrument of his teaching. His major role was that of enlightening their minds and purifying their hearts.

We want powers but we have little awareness of their tremendous price. I dare say that most of us would find ourselves appallingly poor in meeting their requirements.

It should be dearly stated that there is no wisdom in seeking powers and even less in using them. It is a very dangerous path, as more often than not, the aspirant becomes unbalanced and loses far more than he gains.

Valid and legitimate powers are those which result as a bonus from contemplative discipline and expanding insight, but are never displayed.

Even though there are no miracles in a literal sense, we can make our lives miraculous by rehearsing a selected and joyful scene until it objectifies in our life.

Having experienced a few times that which is ultimate to the human condition, "Union With Our Source," the true nature of reality is revealed to be astonishingly different from that which is perceived by our senses. With this monumental and inexplicable awakening comes the universe-shaking knowledge of the true nature of ourselves, of all existence, and of our mysterious Source. Only in this light can miracles be seen and assessed for that which they truly are: the natural consequence of laws of a higher order. When these are understood and are repeatable, they join the ranks of science such as electric power, the telephone, radio, television, astronomy and interplanetary travel.

Man himself and his experience in the universe is a true miracle, the comprehension of which is beyond the reach of our intellectual frequencies. But the explanation of these mysteries can open our mind to a cosmic perspective. The wonder, dear friend, is our natural endowment of the faculties and powers to make of our lives whatever we will. May our minds be filled with love and beauty, contribution and satisfaction.

People are the portals through which men pass into positions
of power and leadership.

— Dr. Paul Parker

151

The Magic of the Mind

Space – Time

Man experiences a kind of optical delusion of his consciousness.
Past, present and future are illusion.
Don't be deluded by the appearance of things.

— Albert Einstein

Our sensory faculties are entirely unable to discern in our environment the uncommonly subtle, the infinitesimal, or the infinitely vast. The delusion of time as "passing" and space as "something" are deeply rooted in our perception. Generally, they evoke no curiosity and we take for granted that things are as they appear.

To the deeply analytical mind, this elusive pair has long been an enigma, and it has elicited volumes of hypotheses and conjecture. Still, modern science is not satisfied with its answers; somehow, they do not seem to fit the equations.

This is not a new quest of research; the same puzzle and confusion has for thousands of years disturbed the sleep of those who would solve its mystery. Yet then, as now, the answer was in their midst. How is this possible? Who among us is so outstandingly learned, so intellectually brilliant as to have solved this monumental riddle?

As is sometimes the case, we are asking the wrong questions. One need only to have asked the contem-platives, those scattered few to whom the mysteries of the nature of all existence have been revealed in their disciplines of long and profound silence.

There is evidence that true insight into the greatest mysteries long predated the earliest extant writings on the subject. Mystical legends, verses and songs were passed down for millenia before the advent of writing. There are quite a number of such records preceeding biblical times. And the Bible, itself a compilation of mystical writings from cover

153

to cover, explains these elusive truths in profusion, but they are concealed in order to protect the unprepared seeker.

Though many scientists still wrestle with the problem of space-time, there are enlightened seekers in every generation who have experienced the highest mysteries, in transcendent union with our Source. It has long been known that time does not pass. We mistake for its passing the movement of forms, the changing from light to dark, the revolving seasons and the seemingly elapsed time between events. Space is equally elusive, but these are essential illusions. Without their appearance it would be quite impossible to function as organized and interacting societies, though some isolated groups still have no need of either calendar or clock.

Actually, time is nonexistent and there is no separation between past, present and future, but in order to experience the human condition they must appear as distinct, one from the other, as a linear ribbon of motion.

Our confusion about the nature of so-called time lies in the inability of our faculties to perceive and distinguish the difference between manifest existence and the cosmic screen of consciousness upon which it is reflected in "the eternal present." Dr. Raynor C. Johnson said, "Space and time become elusive concepts in the microcosm. The changeless amid the changing, the eternal in the midst of time, the ONE amid the many."

Time is an endless documentary of events being projected upon a movie screen, while our perception is that of only one frame at a time. It is the same with space-time; the part cannot be properly identified as separate from the whole.

The mystery is actually much greater than it appears. We are trying to fit the round peg of an unknown into the square hole of a scientific equation which is itself deluding. The enigma lies in our false assumption that things are as they appear. Once we have identified the elements, their arrangements, processes and associations, we feel that we have resolved the problem and are on solid ground. But we have failed even to ask the most important question: what is its true nature? We do not even see the need for this question. Are not the phenomenon and its composition sufficient? The answer is, not if we would know the most significant truth about the object of our study.

My humble apologies to science, about which I know little. My insight lies not in intellectually acquired knowledge, but from a discipline of profound silence, in which limiting mental frequencies are transcended and the true nature of reality reveals itself—far beyond any trace of personality or even the universe. It is the same principle as that of a spacecraft blasting out of the constraints of the earth's gravity and into the freedom of another orbit, except that it is a spherical expansion rather than an empowered liftoff.

One of the revelations resulting from union with the highest source of all existence was that of a "multidimensional universe." This is also true of ourselves.

More significantly, we and all else are a mysterious miracle in action.

Clearly, in matters of the earth plane, we must proceed by its governing laws, but they will serve us only in its lowest dimension of density.

Abstractions such as space-time and the nature of reality require observance of the laws of their dimension. Here, the direction is from the objective effect to its subjective cause, and further still to the nature of its source.

In keeping with the laws of this dimension we must think and speak of time as past, present and future. But the long-trodden path toward the mysteries of the subtle planes and the nature of reality is that of the opposite direction: The lone journey from the surface mind into the retreating depths of silence; the uncharted way from the blinding darkness of the day toward the true light through the inner portal.

155

The wisest minds of whom there is any record had little or no formal education. Their wisdom did not derive from intellectual brilliance, but from revelations of "direct knowing" in their long disciplines of the deepest silence. Ideally, the scientist and the contemplative should dialogue. Highly valuable and beneficial results could result from this exchange.

To understand the answer to space-time, the most direct route is the "backward turning method," using the mind to transcend itself in order to reach into the highest frequences of "direct knowing."

Time is the image of eternity.

— Plato

Revising the Past

A change of impression results in a change of expression.

— Neville Goddard

Though our reason would find it incredulous, by activating the laws of revision we can change the influence of that which has already occurred.

As explained elsewhere, all our mental activity and experiences are recorded in our subconscious mind. Unless revised, they continue to influence our ongoing present. If their nature and quality is life-enhancing, we feel a sense of well-being. If they are in conflict with natural law and order, their energy patterns create stresses, blockages and discomfort.

Happily, we are naturally endowed with the faculty of revision, which can redirect and harmonize the forces resulting from past experience. The following example will illustrate the process:

Neville Goddard, the late mystical philosopher, author and teacher known publicly only as Neville, relates in his book *Resurrection* the story of a young child whose face was seriously burned. According to her well-qualified doctor, she would be badly scarred for life. Her parents, beset with this traumatic grief, accepted this as final and sank into despair.

But the child's grandmother, who adored her, was taking classes with Neville, whose broad teaching included the practical use of laws of revision. Armed with this knowledge, she refused to go to the hospital to see the child, but instead, practiced a daily discipline of ignoring the accident by holding a vision of the child's beautiful and perfect face before her. She groomed her thoughts and emotions to a sense of the highest joy and celebration as she mentally watched her play and amuse herself with her toys.

Both morning and night the grandmother sat quietly and experienced the love and wonder of seeing the child's exceptionally beautiful face and skin. Throughout the day she reinforced the vision of perfection with the happiest of thoughts and emotions. She neither accepted or rejected the doctor's view of permanent disfigurement; instead, she activated the powerful creative forces of imaginal experience with her vision of the child's ultimate beauty and perfection. Aware that the higher her sense of joy, the more masterful the effect, she refused to talk to the distressed parents about the matter. When they called, she quickly changed the subject, saying that she was doing something positive and did not wish to discuss it. They did not understand and thought her cold and insensitive.

After a shorter-than-expected stay in the hospital, the child's mother called to say that the bandages had just been removed and the doctor was awestruck at seeing a perfect face with not a trace of a scar. He announced that only a miracle could account for the perfection of her face.

The magical powers of the creative process, which can change not only our present and so-called future, but even that of the past, lie in unbroken concentration upon joyous fulfillment.

Once something has occurred, we cannot remove the fact that it happened, but we can modify the result by activating laws of a higher order. As all existence is structured in a multidimensional universe, so are the laws and forces of each. Yet, we need not possess the knowledge of a scientist to invoke the laws of our nature. Naturally, the more knowledge, the more control and the higher the success; thus is the noble art of science.

But is it not interesting that thousands of years before the emergence of science, these laws were known and understood? As wisdom is a higher order of knowledge, the greater the wisdom, the less the higher laws were invoked. Due to the lack of general knowledge, the effects of their intervention were and are called miracles. However, to one in control it is a matter of expanded awareness.

158

There are many cases where medical science has attributed healings to the realm of miracles, as that branch of science is not yet familiar with principles and laws of this superior order, though they are fast expanding their frontiers.

But the purpose of this endeavor is to point out that all existence is objectified mind, and that by changing the focus of our attention, conditions are altered.

If we accept things as permanent and unalterable, they will remain so; but if we deprive a negative condition of our energizing attention and practice seeing it differently, it will change according to our ability to remain focused on the desired result as present, and the degree of emotional energy we engender.

It could be said that mind is the architect, while feeling is the moving force. But as with all forces, they have their opposing correspondences. We must be very certain that our energies are directed toward only that which is life and harmony enhancing. Heaven help the one who attempts to use the natural laws to harm others, for the quality of our thoughts is the quality of our experience.

It is tremendously significant that our mind can and does affect the well-being of others. So if we would wish for another an ideal condition of any kind, we should practice thinking of and seeing the person not as they are, but in the ideal. This is the greatest possible gift.

As some measure of reason must be observed, one should not attempt to restore life from the grave or to reverse other laws in conflict with the natural order of progression. We should be aware that effective prayer is not in asking some assumed outside power to change any situation, but in *rejoicing that the desired condition is now present, and remaining faithful to this assumption.*

In summary, identify with the presence of your life-enhancing desire—regardless of appearances—and groom your thoughts, feelings and actions to reflect this position.

Appropriating the feeling of the wish fulfilled is the way to the realization of your desire.

— Neville Goddard

Infinite Supply

Declare strength for weakness, let a weak man say, 'I am strong.'

— Jesus Christ

We are innately endowed to activate limitless and all-pervading energy to our purposes. We are submerged, as it were, in an infinite ocean of powerful forces that await the subtle molding and sculpting of our thoughts, fantasies and imagination.

We are preoccupied with mastering our environment, yet for the most part we are still unaware of the means of self-empowering the required energies for fulfilling our desires.

It is by learning the principles and laws of the creative process of our mind that we find ourselves to be natural creators endowed with all the faculties necessary to initiate energies equivalent to the accomplishment of our goals.

Miraculously, we need not concern ourselves with the "how" of any endeavor. If we will fill our mind and emotions with the joy and excitement of our dream as already realized, then in imagination, do in the silence of our mind all that we would be doing were it already present, "the how" will find its way into the mind. Not only will "the way" present itself, but we will be prompted by some inner motivation to do precisely the right thing at the right time to assure ideal results.

Interestingly a small, three letter word, **HOW,** so often blocks our passage to achievement.

Have you not felt that you would like to do something if only you had the energy? Yes, we have all experienced this illusion. Unaware of the functioning of our mind we falsely assume that we must first feel the strength before beginning the action. Actually, it is the other way around. Charles Simmons wrote: "Realize the power of the human mind on the

161

human body. Mental attitudes are the greatest source of power. Thoughts are the powerhouse."

Before beginning any project, we should prepare our faculties by clearly defining our desire in its ultimate fulfillment, and feel its realization, for the extent of our forces equates with our subconscious conditioning. If we have frequent thoughts of fatigue and a lack of energy, they are perpetuating their own likeness. The way to abundant energy is through our imagination. If we will experience in the silence of our mind that which we would like to be doing and make a habit of this practice, our energies will be equivalent to the magnitude of our desire.

The failure to engage in some desire for lack of energy is to be unaware of our infinite source of supply.

We are marvelously equipped by our thought processes and ability to embody the fulfillment of our desires to achieve anything in the natural order of life.

No thought should be given to the matter of energy, but only to the joy of the fulfilled desire. By making this a daily practice, we are programming our super-ingenious subconscious computer to provide all the energy required to realize our desire.

To belabor our lack of strength for doing that which we would like to undertake is to give cross signals to our source of supply, which neutralizes its response.

Believe that you possess significant reserves of health, energy and endurance and your belief will create the fact.

— William James

Solutions

Man is not the creature of circumstances.
Circumstances are the creatures of men.

— Benjamin Disraeli

Together with millions of other women all over the world, Martha B. hated housework. With three children in school, she constantly complained to her husband that all she did was to shop, cook, clean and launder—endlessly. She was always exhausted, tired when she went to bed and tired when she got up. Though she loved her children, she was frequently cross and they responded by being quarrelsome. There was no affection in the home and everyone suffered. Little wonder that her husband stopped off at the bar on his way home and was often late for dinner. It was not a happy situation, but one all too familiar to many housewives.

One day Martha received a letter from another mother announcing "A Way Out." Betty, an enterprising housewife who had found herself in the same position, began to look on the positive side for a solution to this common problem. She and two of her friends discussed various ideas and settled on one that they chose to explore. They asked the school principal if the mothers could meet at the school each Saturday to implement the ways and means of improving their common lot. The principal consulted the school board and it was agreed that it could be a highly useful community effort.

Betty had done her homework and proved to be a great organizer. All the mothers were invited to participate. At first Martha thought of it as just another duty, but she went to the meeting out of curiosity. To her surprise, she heard Betty and her two friends relating a home life very similar to her own. When the other mothers were asked if anyone else could identify with the same problems, every hand in the large room rose. Asked if they would like to participate in a program for improving matters, they all were enthusiastic.

163

First it was agreed that the Saturday meetings at the school would continue and the following provisions were made: The school gym, restrooms and playground would be made available from ten to four o'clock. Volunteers were asked to head food services, playground, nursery, solutions, entertainment, hobbies, hotline and finances. Each group coordinator asked for volunteers for her committee, and the community project was underway.

Out of a desperate need, both the home mother and the working mother were benefited by having a weekly open forum where they could discuss their problems and help each other with solutions. Visiting specialists were invited to speak on subjects relating to family needs. By taking turns with childcare, each mother now had up to six hours of free time every week, and many enterprising ones arranged for exchange care at other times. They learned how to organize their home duties with efficient streamlining that relieved most of their stress and fatigue. This gave them time for hobbies and workshops at the school on Saturdays, and the opportunity to make friends or demonstrate leadership. They received emotional support through helping each other cope with their common problems, and developed a more positive approach to all areas of their lives.

Some of the teaching and administrative staff had children whom they cheerfully entered in the program. In less than a year, the prindpal announced that both behavior and grades had noticeably improved. And the mothers agreed that their "Way Out" learning, socializing and childcare program worked wonders on the home front.

If there are conditions in your life that need attention, please begin with the idea that you have found the ideal solution; start feeling better about it. Sit down quietly and allow your thoughts to play over the way you would like things to be. Imagine that they are so, and be sure that everyone involved will be benefited by your desire. A few minutes a day of this practice will soon result in a solution.

Perhaps you would like to start a mutual service group. If so, see it functioning. Silently experience the role you would like to play, and its benefits.

Don't wait until you find the time, the mood or the energy; begin in your thoughts NOW and the rest will follow.

Imagination is more important then knowledge.

— **Albert Einstein**

The Magic of the Mind

Knowledge and Wisdom

We can be knowledgeable with other men's knowledge,
but we cannot be wise with other men's wisdom.

— Michel de Montaigne

How beautifully Monsieur de Montaigne garmented this truth. Most of us tend to use knowledge interchangeably with wisdom, yet the two may never have met. The same is true of intelligence and education; they may also be total strangers. Let us look at the two more closely and see how knowledge and wisdom relate.

First, knowledge presupposes many years of serious academic study, resulting in an uncommon degree of expertise in some specialized field. It may embrace an impressively wide base, ingenious resourcefulness and extensive skills. It is indeed of great value, and who would not wish a generous portion? Yet knowledge does not assure a balanced perspective, integrity, morality or compatibility. It may not encompass teamwork, a long-range view, compassion, or tolerance. Neither may it exhibit equilibrium, health, or harmony with the natural order of life. Still, towering high above the norm, extensive knowledge is much to be admired in the activities of worldly gain.

Wisdom, long predating history and education, does not rely solely upon the intellectual faculties; in disciplines of long years of profound silence the mind is used to transcend itself. This enables perception to reach into the higher frequencies of "revelation and direct knowing." All is knowable in the depths of silence.

Dedicated and committed aspirants to the highest truths usually follow one of two paths. Some gather in remote seclusion around an enlightened sage who guides their long years of profound silence to the metaphorical "mountain top" and their further years of integration with their universe-shaking revelations.

167

Those who choose the path of solitude spend long silent years alone in some distant and unfrequented hideaway, until "knowing knew" that it was timely to return to the world in selfless service. The incredible hardships that the latter once endured—without possessions, comfort, shelter or adequate food—took a heavy toll. Many were unable to endure the rigors and sufferings for that which is considered the most elusive and difficult of all endeavors. These are among the demands of wisdom, that mysterious "pearl of great price."

To paraphrase: It is better to stand in the shadow of wisdom than in the sunlight of the unawakened. This is confirmed in the Appocrapha: "If you find a man of wisdom, let your feet wear the steps of his door." With some insight into its depths and the almost insurmountable hardships of its attainment, it is not surprising that wisdom is exalted above knowledge as that of a higher order. According to some of the biblical sages, it was considered the most precious of any possible achievement, to be desired more than any possession: "With all thy getting, get wisdom and get insight."

The planes in which the most profound mysteries are concealed transcend the frequencies of the intellectual faculties; no amount of study or discussion can reach their revealing light. This distinguishes the truly illumined saint or sage from those who are intellectually taught, though each has its place in the great progression.

In viewing the distinction between knowledge and wisdom, it could be rightly said that the former concerns itself with the laws, processes, functions and progress pertaining to the so-called physical dimension of manifest existence. The latter addresses the mysteries of the true nature, purpose, process and source of man and the universe. In particular, the path of wisdom is directed toward the nature of the source from which all existence derives. As stated in the Upanishads of ancient India concerning the mysteries: "Truth lies beyond the known and beyond the unknown."

Among the signs of wisdom we should expect a smooth and quiet harmony between the light of insight and its manifest expression. Its evidence should be less in words and more in the quality of being. The man of wisdom would selflessly and modestly exhibit all the virtues, making himself available to those who would follow his guidance. He would be exemplary in all his conduct, treating everyone and all living things with kindness and respect. He would have no possessions beyond perhaps his simple clothing; he would accept neither money nor gifts other than a token flower, a piece of fruit, or possibly some handmade gift of love such as a warm shawl or a cushion for his comfort.

There would not be a trace of ego or arrogance, of jealousy or envy. His single purpose is the well being and advancement of his followers toward the light. He is at once wise and simple and laughs spontaneously at natural amusements. He sees beauty, poetry and the dance of life beyond the faculty of sight; he hears the music of the universe beyond the sense of sound; he experiences oneness with all manifest existence beyond any human faculty. Though there might be no visible display, he would be not only loving but love itself.

Lao-Tzu, one of the greatest examples of wisdom refined into simplicity, said: "By some he was considered to be a simpleton, which was in fact his only merit."

Having walked together through this brief glimpse of knowledge and wisdom, I leave it to you, dear friend, to discern the significance between the two.

*Here the heart may give a useful lesson to the head,
and learning, wiser grow without his books.*

— William Cowper

Destiny in the Making

The unbeatable combination: the man of head and heart.

— H. Heine

A remarkable example of the creative process of our mind is the story of Joseph, a little Eastern European boy whose mother died when he was only five. At eleven he was fully orphaned. Having no one to care for him, he supported and educated himself from this time forward.

Fascinated with books and eager to learn, he mastered German, French and English while still a young teenager, and devoured the classics of these three cultures in addition to his own. But above all, he dreamed of living some day in that far-away wonderland called America, the home of his dearest and most intimate friends, Mark Twain's Tom Sawyer and Huckleberry Finn.

When he grew up, he managed to get as far as Paris and while walking the streets of this city to conserve bus fare, he passed daily by a new excavation site where the famous Coty Cosmetic Company was preparing to build its new headquarters. Day by day, with empty pockets, he would stop to watch the work in progress. To brighten his mood, he began to imagine that the entire project was "his"; as the handsome building rose, he secretly identified himself as its proud owner.

This new thought pattern so lifted his spirits that he soon improvised on a shoestring the most modest of business ventures.

Always dreaming far beyond all reason and logic, he now identified himself as a highly successful international manufacturer and his affairs grew and expanded many times over.

While continuing his education in night classes at Paris's Sorbonne University, he lived greatly in his fantasies and his daydreams.

171

One day, moved by the muses of inspiration, he inquired about larger new quarters, and was astonished and excited to learn that the Coty Cosmetic Company was now consolidating its operation in the suburbs of Paris and was about to put on the market the handsome building of his earlier dreams. Now, having acquired substantial finances, he bought the building at once and paid for it in cash. On moving in, he celebrated that his penniless dream of ownership had crystallized into fact.

Continuing his waking dreams, Joseph acquired other buildings on both sides of the Atlantic. His business affairs expanded into international scope and he now maintained three homes on two continents.

This unprotected orphan child had developed himself into a respected position in several foreign countries and enjoyed a full and enriching life—all because he lived in his imagination, his fantasies and dreams of the day.

I know this story very well indeed. For when we met at a formal luncheon in Paris, this handsome and distinguished man engaged me in a happy conversation and then excused himself and disappeared briefly.

Later, he told me that he had gone to ask our hostess to seat him beside me. And there began a beautiful and exciting storybook romance.

However, Joseph, having fulfilled his lifelong dream of living in America, was settled in New York, while I was happily situated in Los Angeles.

When we each returned home to opposite sides of the continent, there began a steady westward stream of flowers, telephone calls and letters, punctuated by occasional visits. Now, another of his enduring dreams was that of an ideal marriage and he had decided almost from our first meeting that I was to be that ideal mate. He urged me to move to New York but you can well understand my reluctance to exchange California sunshine and year-round roses for the icy winds and snow of New York. I resisted, but Joseph persisted and in time his noble and endearing character grew in my affections. So I went to New York, lived at the Barbizon Hotel for Women and attended nearby Hunter College.

When first I arrived in the city I saw from my hotel windows a veritable fairyland of snow-white splendor. Walking through the dazzling spectacle of Central Park for the first time in the enchantment of softly falling snowflakes, I was unprepared for a scene that was so spellbinding that it appeared unreal. Every tree, bush and growing thing was costumed as for an ethereal ballet, with raiments of snowy white jewels that sparkled and shimmered in the morning sunlight. Strolling hand in hand with my love, we visited the zoo, the large poetic fountain and the boat lake, all arrayed in splendor. It was majestic.

I enjoyed my college studies and the city's rich repertoire of the arts. The broad array of the world's finest concert artists, the ballet, the theater and the wealth of treasures in the museums provided enrichment for twenty-five years. At that time I never guessed that I would join the ranks of the speakers I enjoyed at Town Hall, the universities, The New School for Social Research, and all around me.

But I have digressed from my story and I hasten to return to the affairs of the heart, to the one I most loved and admired in all the world.

I came to recognize that my own dream of some "Undefined Wonder" was crystallizing in our approaching union. His dream of an ideal marriage materialized; we were the happiest, most devoted of sweethearts for the remaining twenty-one years of his blessed life. It was a marriage made in heaven; everyday, we took long walks together hand-in-hand. And throughout the years when he had to be in Europe for a month at a time, or when we lived in Paris and he came to America for several weeks, we each wrote loveletters every day. He said that my loving thoughts and constant praise were the inspiration and highlight of his day. Clearly, he had climbed the tree of life on the branches of dreams and fantasy.

The Magic of the Mind

Your world in every detail is your consciousness objectified.

— Neville Goddard

Paris Project

Mental attitude is the greatest source of power.

— Charles Simmons

Elsewhere I have noted that my late husband climbed the tree of life on the branches of dreams and fantasy. But the last of his dreams time did not allow him to fulfill: that of relocating our French business headquarters to another part of Paris and finding a single tenant for our seven-floor Paris office building. Reflecting over his last dream I wanted to fulfill it in his memory. However, I was exceedingly busy with his European and American business responsibilities and the management of our New York office building in addition to preparing and delivering twice-weekly lectures and television programs.

I knew that if all conditions and timing were perfect, there should result a handsome gain; otherwise, there was the risk of a substantial loss. After careful consideration, I decided to undertake this project as well. I began to invoke the principles and laws of the creative process of the mind by assuming that the entire plan was already complete and mutually rewarding. Every night for the following three weeks, I rehearsed imaginary scenes and conversations confirming this effect. I then left for Paris, arriving at my apartment in the evening. No one knew the purpose of my trip, there were no discussions, letters, telephone calls, wires or requests. Yet, incredible as it seems, at nine o'clock the next morning, my secretary announced a caller who said, "Madame Berlay, if you will consider moving your business headquarters elsewhere and lease me your entire building, I will pay all your moving costs and any expense of preparing your new location."

Imagine. I had barely arrived; with the time change between Paris and New York, it was for me three o'clock in the morning. So with less than one full night's sleep, already the most important part of my plan was accomplished.

I then asked the real estate agent next door to find us a new location, requesting, among other things, one spacious floor with lots of big windows, together with a private apartment for my frequent visits. He said, 'The apartment will make it impossible to find— there is no such thing."

After much persuasion, he said, "Very well, Madame, when do you need all this?" I answered with some embarrassment, as I knew that such things move very slowly in Europe, "Within three weeks, as I must be back to my lectures in New York by then."

Well, the agent leaned back in his big chair and laughed heartily at my naivete. "Surely," he went on, "you can't be serious. Give me six months and I may be able to help you."

I thanked him cheerfully and said I was sure he would have something to show me by that afternoon. Within a couple of hours, he took me to two locations. The first, I rejected at a glance, but the second I knew was custom-made from my creative dream rehearsals. Facing the street was one hundred feet of enormous arched windows twelve feet high. The place had all my specifications, including a lovely private apartment.

So after a thorough inspection and evaluation, we went directly to the owner where we concluded the affair. The agent stood awestruck; never had he seen so quick a decision or earned his commission so easily.

The multifaceted project was complete, not in six months as the agent had projected, but in less than eight hours. And it was conceived and developed from a mental blueprint that I had designed on the opposite side of the Atlantic.

As stated elsewhere, repetition of the *consequences* of your fulfilled desire, together with your highest joyful emotion, are essential to building up the energy that the subconscious requires to develop your visionary negatives into strong prints. Only when this has been achieved can the creative process project them into your outer world.

Remember that your subconscious has no faculties for assessing time, space or "how to." Just as a camera records its subject "as is," so does your subconscious accept and reproduce your thoughts, emotions, assumptions and beliefs as they are.

And it matters not whether your project is at hand or at a far distance. National borders, foreign languages, or complex circumstances are no obstacle to the creative process, nor are the ways and means by which things occur. The HOW is its responsibility, and if we are practicing properly we are experiencing the finished product, the end result. If in our mind our desire is already realized, it follows that we cannot be concerned with how it will occur.

Of great significance are the words of Neville Goddard, the beautiful soul after whom our son was named: 'Think not OF your goal, which positions it in the future, but FROM it, which places it in the past.

"Your world," he said, "is in every detail, your consciousness objectified. Nothing comes from without; all comes from within. A change of feeling is a change of destiny."

Do you see the magic of our minds? Truly, we can create "miracles," and I've invoked a few, if we will begin by assuming that our desire is already fulfilled and practice doing in our imagination that which we would be doing were it already realized.

Man is the architect of circumstances.

— **G. H. Laws**

The French Riviera

The silent experience of success is half way there.

— The Author

After spending several weeks in Spain, I decided to pass the remaining weeks of one summer in Cannes, France, and prepared to leave by car. After telling a resident friend of my departure, she began to cry and begged me to stay. She and others said, "Don't be foolish; you will arrive on the French Riviera on their greatest holiday, the fourteenth of July, when the overcrowded city is bursting its seams. There will be not a hotel room or apartment to rent within thirty miles of the beach. You will be forced to sleep in your car if you are lucky enough to find a place to park."

I knew I must do some serious creative imagining that night if I was to find suitable accommodations in Cannes. I mentally rehearsed, in vivid and happy detail, the pleasures of a beautiful apartment on the top floor of one of the loveliest buildings ringing the Cannes Bay. It looked down on the blue Mediterranean, where I swam daily and promenaded along the picturesque beach. So incredibly real was my practice that the next morning I cheerfully and confidently announced that I would be leaving in an hour.

The friend who lived nearby was inconsolable, so I said, "Pack your bags and come along." She answered, "But my fourteen-year-old son, I can't leave him alone." "Bring him," I answered, realizing that the two would complicate my plans. So off we went to the famous and elegant playground of the jet set of the Western World.

Knowing it would be useless to inquire at the regal Hotel Carlton where I had stayed a few weeks earlier, or the other fine hotels along the Croisette, I inquired at a small but lovely hotel one block from the beach, and incredibly, a guest was just checking out. "But only one night," said the firm concierge. So we had a great suite overlooking the blue bay where we enjoyed a delightful breakfast on the terrace.

Realizing that we must check out within three or four hours, I left early to visit the real estate offices for apartment rentals. When I explained that I needed at least three bedrooms on a high floor along the Croissette, everybody laughed. Not for love nor money, they assured me, was there one vacant apartment in the entire city of Cannes, as well as for many miles around. Undaunted, I thanked them cheerfully and went on my way to the next agent. After six agencies had laughed with roars of amusement at my naiveté, I saw that it was up to me to fulfill my own dream.

This is the point at which a seeming obstacle to our plans triggers the self-programmed negatives in our subconscious, which then begin to send up messages of doubt, fear, failure and disappointment. Immediately our spirits are invaded by all these conflicting forces—reminiscent of a football team of dauntless heavyweights running interference against our plans. And it is here that knowledge and experience are vital.

Recognizing all these signs I immediately thought of the guests whom I had invited from Paris and New York and wondered where and how I would house them. But I quickly recognized the situation that confronted me and began silently to *celebrate the ideal apartment in which we were all happily settled. I put on a happy face and strolled lightly down the avenue, pretending that all was wonderful and that I was leisurely returning home. Noting the lovely curve of the bay, I allowed it to attract my feet in that direction.*

So I walked toward the building which I found the most attractive and, courting the joy of fulfillment, I pretended that I lived there. Cheerfully confident, I went around to the back of the building and found the small quarters of the concierge but she was nowhere to be seen. After a little walk, I returned just as she appeared.

Sustaining the bright feelings and manner of my position I asked her cheerfully not merely for a three-or four-bedroom apartment, but I stipulated the top floor, adding that I needed it at once and that I expected to stay for two months.

"Well, you are very lucky, Madame," she said, "for one of our tenants just moved out unexpectedly and I was up there cleaning the apartment."

In less than an hour, the three of us were happily installed in a beautiful three-bedroom apartment with a terrace on the top floor overlooking acres of formal rose gardens and the famous Cannes marina with its abundance of opulent yachts.

My friend and her son from Spain stayed with me for a week and were replaced by other friends from Paris. We had only to cross the flower- and tree-lined street and walk through the rose gardens to swim in the iridescent blue waters of the Mediterranean.

Reflecting over these recent weeks, I saw that this had been one of many lovely summers that was started in thought, rehearsed in imagination, and out-pictured broadly in the four directions. It was a delightful holiday despite predictions to the contrary.

Once you have adequately imprinted your subconscious with your desired blueprint, all other conditions will bend to the laws of the mind. The real estate offices in Cannes, for example, were stating absolute facts; there was nothing to rent within thirty miles of the city. But I had self-programmed a very pleasant summer, and the thought seeds that I planted in New York, bloomed brightly on the Spanish and French Rivera's.

*The Qybalion: transcend and transmute by identifying
with conditions which evoke laws of a higher order.*

Love Story

To love for the sake of being loved is human,
but to love for the sake of loving is angelic.

— Alphonse de Lamartine

A classic example of the quality of our dominant thought patterns being the quality of our experience is that of Donna, who was deeply in love, and engaged to marry, a man of admirable character and intelligence. But after a lover's quarrel, she broke the engagement and moved to a far away state where she foolishly thought the great distance and new surroundings would help her to forget and re-establish her life. However, cut off from family and friends, and thinking only of the man she still loved, she found herself drowning in sorrow.

With no interest in making new friends, her life consisted only of home and work. This pattern became so strongly imprinted in her subconscious mind that for the next twenty years she led an uneventful and lonely existence. Reading was her only pleasure and she devoured at least a book a week.

One evening as Donna watched the news, she was shocked to see the man she loved attending the funeral services for his wife. (He had later married and become a prominent public figure.) Her heart pounded and her emotions ran wild on seeing him again. It seemed as if the intervening years had not occurred, for her love was as deep and alive as ever. She could think of nothing else and wanted to call him but didn't dare.

Reflecting over the matter, Donna decided to listen to the reasons of her heart, which led her to spend every free moment in thoughts of him and their reunion.

Realizing that had she not broken their engagement they would now be married, she fantasized that they really were, and in her imagination she included him in all she did. In her daydreams before leaving for work, she kissed him goodbye and wished him a happy day. She thought of him frequently during her working hours and almost counted the minutes before they would meet again in the evening. At home, she greeted him happily and lovingly, asked about his day and thought only about his pleasure.

Living so strongly in her imagination, where she preoccupied herself in trying to make him happy, Donna was, within a few weeks, transformed into the bright and cheerful person of her former self. In her secret dreams they enjoyed the theatre, concerts, museums, and lovely evenings of dancing as before. She gave fun dinner parties and enjoyed a variety of social events with their friends. Life was beautiful again and everything took on a bright new promise.

Not knowing where it would lead her, she had lived in her happy fantasies for several months when one day Donna saw her beloved's picture in the local newspaper with the announcement that he would address a prominent public function the following week. Again, her heart pounded and her hands trembled as she realized that he would soon be in her city and that she might have a chance to meet with him. Immediately, her thoughts turned to how she could properly and discreetly contact him at the meeting.

As the function was held in a large assembly hall, she would arrive very early and sit in the first row, directly in front of the podium. She would wear a bright-colored dress so he couldn't miss seeing her. But would he recognize her after twenty years? How much had she changed? Would he remember, and if so, would there still be a trace of their love in his heart? Would he want to talk to her? Would he show any sign of recognition, or would she be just another blurred face among hundreds of others in the audience? Such thoughts ran away with her until she recognized that she was defeating her purpose by being entirely negative. She regained her focus and began to rehearse the imaginary scene that she wanted to occur.

Throughout the week, Donna lived every free moment in scenarios of imaginal experience. Assuming that she sat directly in front of him, she imagined that he caught her eye and with a flushed face, he hesitated slightly in his sentence on recognizing her. She saw him glancing back to her repeatedly and felt his eagerness to meet with her at the first possible moment. Over and over, she re-experienced all that she wanted to see and hear—how he hastily sent someone to bring her backstage at the conclusion of his address, his excitement in finding her again, his invitation for dinner, asking for her address and telephone, and his desire to meet with her right after his luncheon with his hosts and the other invited guests.

Not only did Donna re-experience every happy detail of her desire, but her emotions were highly charged with joy and excitement. She knew that this would greatly increase the forces of the creative process, which in turn would influence their meeting.

At last, Saturday morning arrived and she dressed and groomed herself with meticulous care, making a point of leaving early to be assured of a front row seat facing the podium. Happily, she settled into just the seat of her choice and waited spellbound for the program chairman to introduce the honorable guest. As she was the first one in the assembly hall, the waiting seemed interminable. She knew that he must be just backstage and that someone was watching the time for him to appear. If only he knew the surprise that awaited him in the front row.

At last the hall was full and someone walked toward the podium carrying papers of introduction. Donna was breathless. She sensed his nearness and waited for the final words before he would be presented.

Any instant he would step out into view and back, she hoped, into her life. Her excitement mounted, then suddenly, there he was, striding briskly and elegantly toward the podium. Before his first words, his eyes swept across the audience accompanied by his wide and winning smile. He showed no awareness of her presence. Her heart was doing acrobatics and her palms were wet from nervous tension. Her whole future depended upon what occurred at the end of the hour. Donna knew that no one in the audience watched or listened with anything approaching her rapt attention. How marvelous he looked, how confident and persuasive; already the audience had twice applauded his remarks. She noticed the gray at his temples and found it wonderfully attractive and wondered how much she had aged. Would he still find her pretty? Her emotions created waves of energy flowing from head to toe as he made popular and emotionally charged points.

He was in the middle of a sentence, when suddenly he glanced down toward her row, sweeping right past her, then quickly back in clear surprise. He hesitated for a second before finishing his sentence and his face became flushed, as if from the emotional impact.

Donna was stunned, petrified, her mind went blank, everything was in a whirl, she lost all focus. She heard his words, but understood nothing he said for the remainder of the hour. She was conscious only that he kept looking at her and she sensed from his eyes that his feelings for her were still alive. But was she merely imagining that which her heart wanted to see and to feel? Only minutes stood between this great uncertainty and the truth. Her life hung in the balance. She hardly breathed.

At last, she heard him conclude and the program chairman reappeared and shook his hand as the audience stood in wild applause. Donna thought she stood too, but she couldn't remember applauding—she felt not even the strength to move.

The two men disappeared behind the curtain and Donna stood stunned as the audience began to leave the hall. Suddenly someone touched her arm and said that the speaker would like her to come backstage. Taking her arm, he led her through a side door into a room where several people were gathered around him in excited animation. Upon her entrance, she heard him say, "Excuse me for a moment, gentlemen," and taking a few brisk steps in her direction, he reached for her two hands. "I can't believe my eyes," he said softly. "Give me your card quickly, where can I reach you right after lunch?" Donna hadn't said

186

a word. She fumbled in her purse and was so nervous that she spilled its contents all over the floor. Lipstick rolled in one direction, compact in another and her cards scattered over the room. Suddenly, half-a-dozen men scurried about retrieving the mysterious contents of a lady's purse. The moment seemed frozen, then they walked outside. He asked if she was driving or if he could get her a cab. He closed her door and the car sped away. She never remembered how she got home, but somehow there she was in her apartment with her eyes blankly glued to the telephone. Waiting for his call, the time seemed neither long nor short, it simply was not registering in her dazed mind.

She was vaguely aware that he did not know whether or not she was married, if she had children or anything about her present status. He could not know how she felt about him. Would there still be hurt, resentment or anger over their lover's quarrel? She was sure that he would at least be curious and glad to share some thoughts about the intervening years.

Still lost in her thoughts and emotions, the telephone rang and her heart leaped to answer. He was all finished with his engagement and could he grab a cab and come right over?

Breathlessly answering the door she wondered if it were not another episode of her dream rehearsals as he walked in, placed his two hands upon her shoulders and asked, "Why did you go away? Why didn't you let me know where you were? I went through hell when you disappeared. But that's the past and this is now; tell me about you. Are you married? Have you been married? Have you any children? What have you done all these years? Tell me," he blurted out, all in one breath.

Donna explained how very deeply she had regretted having run away; how she had suffered for twenty years for her foolish action. "We won't look back," he said, "but you must return home. Promise you will, as soon as possible. We must begin where we left off.

I never stopped wondering where you were and what you were doing all these years. Thank God, I've found you at last," he sighed, as he drew her close and held her ever so lovingly. That night they talked long and late about the intervening years during which his life had been so full and hers so empty.

David told her of his heartache when she left, how it had affected his work, as he was unable to concentrate; how, with his spirit so low, so crushed, it was only with the greatest effort that he had forced himself to somehow muddle through. He had tried every way he could think of to find her, to tell her that a lover's quarrel was not worth the dreadful suffering that he assumed she, too, was experiencing in her hideaway. He explained that it was the most painful time of his life and that his wounds seemed never to heal.

Donna was shocked. How, she wondered aloud, could she ever have been so selfish, so insensitive to his feelings? She had thought only of her pain, her pride and resentment. Never once had she thought of David as suffering. She had no idea of the grief she had caused him. Had she guessed she would have called, they would have talked and all would have been resolved. How blinding is ignorance, she confessed, how disastrous pride and resentment.

After both had unburdened their hearts — it seemed that all the pent-up emotion had to be relieved—David asked Donna to promise him that she would return home soon, that they might begin again as devoted sweethearts with a bright and promising future.

The following day Donna drove David to the airport. Suddenly, in less than twenty-four hours, everything had grown more beautiful; they both noticed it. It was as though some invisible obstruction had vanished from their sight and they saw the enchanting beauty of nature that had been there all the while. This time they parted with eager anticipation, and David said he would call every night until she returned. The next day Donna resigned from her job, but remained for another month to assist her replacement. She then returned home as excited as a teenager. David met her eagerly and helped her to settle into an apartment. They dated for six months while they each adjusted to their new life, and then had a fashionable and well publicized wedding. Today they are the happiest of couples.

Donna told David that through her suffering she had learned that love stands on two pillars, selfless service and forgiveness.

The heart has reasons, the reason knows not of.

— Blaise Pascal

The Creative Process in Review

All men of action are dreamers.

James Huneker

Of all our attitudes, the most important is that which we hold about ourselves, for it is reflected in our experience. The president or head of a country is playing the role of his self-identification and his sense of self-worth, and the beggar is doing precisely the same thing.

As explained throughout this book, each of us is born with powerful creative faculties for achieving our purpose, but as in all else, we must inform ourselves of their natural principles and laws and learn how to use them.

All attainment has its price—little price, little gain. But if we desire something of a higher value, it requires a higher measure of attention and energy. It is the same process, as there is but one law of creation: sustain fulfillment in the mind and emotions.

If our desire is important to us we should give it daily attention, recalling that a regular and specified time of "imaginal experience" in which we *joyfully rehearse the ultimate expression of our fulfilled desire* builds up energy and heat which in turn matures our mental blueprint. Our imagination *impresses* it upon our subconscious mind, which acts as a nurturing womb for our brainchild, and when it is sufficiently formed and energized, the creative process of our subconscious expresses it into the outer world of our experience.

It is the same principle and process of all living things: idea or thought seed, conception, maturing and birth. All begin in the interplay of the pairs of opposites, equal but opposite energies, beginning in the subjective and ending in the objective.

Be aware that there is a developmental interval between desire and fulfillment. If you feel that your discipline of *impressions* has not resulted in their expected *expression,* you should observe your practice and be certain that you are silently remaining in the end result of your fulfilled desire, and that your rehearsal is always that of doing joyfully what you would be doing were it already objectified. It is also important to look for inspiration in a book or music or some source of your interest before beginning your "creative silence." Inspiration and emotional warmth are necessary to the life-giving process. And of course a relatively easy goal requires less energizing than one of greater magnitude.

You should groom your mind daily to think, act, feel and hear the presence of your desire as already realized. Embody the role and stay in character. As amusingly stated by Norman Vincent Peale, "Dear Lord, let me be the kind of person my dog thinks I am."

So, dear friend, if you would be unsurpassed in your field, head some illustrious organization, own your own prestigious company or be the chairman of the board; if you would increase your income, enjoy robust health or an ideal companion, or if you would harmonize relations, acquire a degree, restore a failing business or live stress-free, you are now marvelously equipped with the wisdom of the world's greatest sages to "begin at the ultimate you desire to attain."

As I bring to a close this communion of our minds I like to think of it as a communion of our spirit, for my heart overflows in full-flowering affection as I hold you, dear one, in my brightest visions.

Lovingly,

Louise Berlay

The Creative Process

"Experience is the mirror of the mind. (First, question whether or not your desire is morally justified. It must not harm or diminish anyone.) —

Louise Berlay, lecturer-author of *The Magic of the Mind.*

ॐ

It takes a person who is wide awake to make his dreams come true."

— Roger Bacon, 1214, English philosopher

ॐ

"Success begins with a dream. Today's dream is tomorrow's reality."

— Shakespeare, 1561, English literary genius, playwright, actor.

ॐ

"All men of action are dreamers."

George Herbert, 1593, English metaphysical poet.

ౠ

"Man can be no greater than his loftiest dreams."

—LB.

ౠ

"He who dreams most achieves most."

"Moses of the Bible dreamed dreams and endured
in seeing the invisible."

ౠ

"We live as we dream."

— Joseph Conrad, 1857, Polish-English novelist.

ౠ

"The greatest of mysteries are concealed within the world dream."

ৎ

"Fully relax and enjoy your creative time. Live it and celebrate it silently in the present. Don't try to make it happen."
— L.B.

ৎ

"All that we see and seem is but a dream within a dream."
— Edgar Allen Poe, 1809, noted American poet and literary figure.

ৎ

"Not facts, but dreams of fancy shape our lives."
— Neville Goddard, Barbadian-American mystic-philosopher.

ৎ

Thomas Edison, noted American inventor of the microphone (precursor of the telephone), and the electric lamp, took frequent short, daily naps and awoke with his solutions.

Playwright, J.B. Priestly dreamed three entire plays in detail.

ॐ

"There is the waking dream of the day and the sleeping dream of the night. Make your waking dream a silent, joyous celebration." — L.B.

ॐ

"If there were dreams to sell, what would you buy "
– Thomas Lovell Beddoes, 1803

ॐ

"As within, so without, as above, so below.
The ancient and legendary Hermes."

ॐ

"Stop trying to make it happen. This creates more wishing and hoping which multiplies and sustains itself. 'Be there now!' Experience your dream as having already occurred. What would you be doing and feeling if these conditions were present? Silently practice doing and feeling these happy consequences!" — L.B.

ॐ

'What we are is the result of all that we have thought."
– The Buddha, Sidartha Gautma, Nepal 563 BC

ॐ

"Learning without thought is labor lost."
K'ung-fu-tsu (Confucius), 551 BC, Great Chinese Sage.

ॐ

"As men think, so are they. Thoughts are the parents of all actions, good
and bad. As he acts, so will be the consequences."
—Dr. Evans-Wentz, late 1800's English mystic-philosophy.
Oxford professor. Many Years in Far East.

ॐ

"Act the role of your choice, feel its presence, stay in character.
Celebrate during every free moment." — **L.B.**

ॐ

"The mind yields fruits corresponding to its thoughts."
— Swami Muktananda, 20th Century mystic of India.

ॐ

"Whether you think you can,
or you think you can't,
you are right."
— Henry Ford, developed first U.S. car.

ॐ

"Nurture your mind with great thoughts.
Experience is the child of thought."
— Disraeli, 1804, English statesman, author.

ॐ

"It is only through concentration that we reach our goals."
— Plotinus, 205 BC, Egyptian-Greek mystic.

ॐ

"Our life is what our thoughts have made it."
—Marcus Auraelius, 121 AD, Roman emperor, philosopher.

ॐ

"Spirit is stronger than any material force.
Thoughts rule the world."
— R.W. Emerson, 1803, philosopher, writer, lecturer.

&

"We are natural, inherent creators. Fix the mind not on desire but on joyful fulfillment now! Stop trying to make it happen. Celebrate! Joyfully throughout all waking hours." — **L.B.**

&

"The quality of our thoughts evoke the laws of their likeness, thus we are self-rewarded, self-denied, self-enriched or self-impoverished." — **L.B.**

&

"Man is not what he thinks he is, but *what he thinks, he is.*"
— R.W. Emerson, American philosopher.

&

"The face is the mirror of the mind, the eyes without speaking, confess the secrets of the heart."
— St. Jerome, c. 347 AD, Christian scholar.

ॐ

"A man is literally what he thinks. He is the complete sum of all his thoughts. All that he achieves and all that he fails to achieve are the direct result of his thoughts."
— James Allen, English author.

ॐ

"Daily check your practice; are you trying to make it happen? Celebrate its presence."
— L.B.

ॐ

"Man is conscious spirit, and what he thinks, as a habit, he experiences. By his every thought and action man creates his own causes that result in his experience."
— L.B.

ॐ

"So long as you are concerned 'by means of,' you will always be depending upon something else."
— Huang-po, ancient Chinese patriarch.

ᘓ

"Every idea carries its own solution."

ᘓ

'Through ignorance, I have imagined the unhappy conditions of my life."
— Ancient East Indian sage.

ᘓ

Man is ruled by habits of his own making. Begin today: if you don't like some aspect of your life, then deny it the sustaining energy of thought and speech." — **L.B.**

ᘓ

"Declare strength for weakness, beginning each man with himself."
— Jesus

ᘓ

'Enjoy to the fullest the resources that are within thy reach."
— Pindar, 518, greatest Greek lyric poet.

ᘓ

"The student is taught to begin at the ultimate
he desires to attain."
— Ancient Chinese sage.

ᘓ

"Imagination bodies-forth the forms of things."
— Shakespeare, 1564, English literary genius.

ᘓ

"Begin at the end result of your desire (not step by step). Embody
ultimate fulfillment, now." — L.B.

ᘓ

"Imagination is more important than knowledge."
— Albert Einstein, 1879, German-American physicist.

ᘓ

'That synthetic and magical power *imagination."*
— Samuel Taylor Coleridge, b:1872, English poet.

ൟ

"Sow a thought and you reap an act,
Sow an act and you reap a habit, Sow a habit and you reap a
character, Sow a character and you reap a destiny."
— Anonymous

ൟ

"The best pupil goes straight to the ultimate."
— Ancient Japanese patriarch.

ൟ

"Yes, and our thoughts body-forth our destiny." — **L.B.**

ൟ

"The shortest interval between desire and fulfillment is *embodied
imagination as present. Desire motivates...
Imagination implements*

And celebrating acceptance manifests. — **L.B.**

ൟ

"Act the part and you will become the part."
— William James, 1842, American philosopher-author.

❧

"Creation emerges from the divine or absolute
imaginal dynamic. *All creation is imagined.*
— Dr. Raynor Johnson, noted English-Australian physicist,
author, lecturer.

❧

"Your achievement shall be in proportion to the
greatness of your desire."
— Evelyn Underhill, 1911, English poet, novelist, Oxford lecturer and
historian of mysticism.

❧

"Yes, and your discipline of embodying and celebrating its fulfillment
in the present." — L.B

❧

"The good or ill of man lies within his own will."
— Epictetus, 50 AD, Phrygian philosopher.

❧

"You can imagine your future."
Henry Kaiser, late 1800's, first built all his ships in imagination.

❧

"Imagination is the only thing that will take us anywhere." —
Vivekananda, 1800's, enlightened sage of India.

❧

'To know is nothing at all.
To imagine is everything."
— Anatole France, 1844, noted French author.

❧

"Without the play of fantasy no creation has
ever come into being."
— Carl Yung, 1875, Swiss psychologist.

❧

"Do not be conformed to this world, but be transformed
by the renewal of your mind."
— The Bible.

ॐ

"Behind the mental faculties the animating power
is constructive imagination."
— Professor Ribot of France.

ॐ

"Practice daily. Be a great actor. No matter what you are doing at the
moment, your chosen self-identity must be its foundation. If your dream
were already realized, how would you feel? Joyfully cultivate and sustain
this self-identity."
— L.B.

ॐ

"Think not of your desire but *from its fulfillment.*
— Neville. Teacher, author, mystic.

ॐ

"In order to change anything in our lives we must begin by changing
some aspect of our thinking, acting and feeling pattern. Most importantly,
we should add fulfillment to our self-image."

ℰ

"The process is not wishing, hoping and expecting which sustains things as they are."

Wrong: "I'm getting better..." "I'm going to..."

Right: Think cheerfully of that which would bring you the greatest pleasure (not the means, such as finances, energy or ability). Imagine, over and over again, that you are experiencing that joyous state or condition. With each practice its mental design is more strongly imprinted in the domain of causes. When it is sufficiently energized it will flower-forth in your objective experience.

I joyfully celebrate the fulfillment of your dearest dreams.

— L.B.

ABOUT THE AUTHOR

Louise Berlay lived for many years between Los Angeles, New York and Paris and has made some sixty trips abroad in all directions. She has taught the creative process widely including Paris, New York and on New York television. She is now settled atop a high-rise at the beach in Southern California

"Our roots lie in majesty, love and beauty," says Louise," and with guidance they will flower radiantly in our lives."

Neville Goddard Books Online

http://www.feelingisthesecret.org/
http://www.atyoucommand.org/
http://www.awakenedimaginationandthesearch.org/
http://www.nevillegoddardfreedomforall.org/
http://www.nevillegoddardoutofthisworld.org/
http://www.prayertheartofbelieving.com/
http://www.nevillegoddardseedtimeandharvest.org/
http://www.thelawandthepromise.com/
http://www.thepowerofawareness.org/
http://www.yourfaithisyourfortune.com/

Additional Metaphysical Resources

http://pistissophiaaudio.com/
http://theiamdiscourses.com/
http://asearchforgod.org/
http://iammeditations.org/
http://christreturns.org/
http://jeshuathepersonalchrist.org/

www.TheSickle.Org
www.TheSharpSickle.Com

www.MetaphysicalPocketBooks.Com
www.Audioenlightenment.Com

CPSIA information can be obtained
at www.ICGtesting.com
Printed in the USA
BVHW061559100719
553094BV00011B/225/P